WELL-CLAD
WINDOWSILLS

TOVAH MARTIN

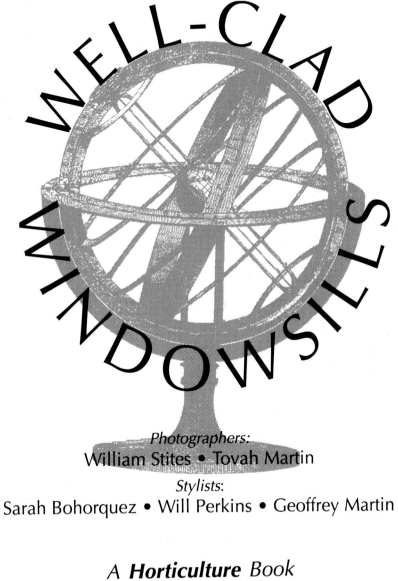

WELL-CLAD WINDOWSILLS

Photographers:
William Stites • Tovah Martin

Stylists:
Sarah Bohorquez • Will Perkins • Geoffrey Martin

A **Horticulture** *Book*
MACMILLAN · USA

To Joy Logee Martin

MACMILLAN • USA
A Prentice Hall Macmillan Company
15 Columbus Circle
New York, New York 10023

A **Horticulture** Book
An affiliate of *Horticulture*, The Magazine of American Gardening

Library of Congress Cataloging-in-Publication Data

Martin, Tovah.
     Well-clad windowsills : houseplants for four exposures / Tovah
  Martin.
        p.   cm.
     "A Horticulture book."
     Includes index.
     ISBN 0-671-85015-6
     1. Window gardening.   2. House plants.   I. Title.
  SB419.M325   1994
  635.9'65—dc20   93-39565

Designed by Levavi & Levavi

Manufactured in the United States of America

10   9   8   7   6   5   4   3   2   1

First Edition

~

Frontispiece: A glass door provides plenty of light for the ivy-leaved pelargoniums 'Sugar Baby' (far left) and 'Desrumeaux' (far right, on pedestal). The sunbeams also nurture Rosmarinus officinalis *trained into standard form and* Oxalis tetraphylla *(formerly O. deppei).*

Front cover: A blushing pink arrangement of Impatiens *'Hawaiian Pink' (right),* Impatiens *'Double Amethyst' (left), and* Streptocarpus *'Light Pink' (left foreground).*

Back cover: In a sunny Gothic window sit a pair of Oxalis ortgiesii *standards with* Oxalis regnellii *'Atropurpurea' (left foreground) and* Oxalis crassipes *'Alba' (right foreground).*

Where would I be without friends and colleagues? One thing is certain—this book would not be sitting before you if it were not for so many people who lent a hand, gave encouragement, and inspired me while I was writing. I owe the greatest debt to my husband, Geoffrey Martin, who carted plants, quelled my fears, proofread, and offered sage advice with never-failing good humor. I would also like to thank my family for their unstinting understanding and advice. I am especially grateful to my parents and sisters, Joy Logee Martin (my mother-in-law), Byron Martin (my brother-in-law), and Richard Logee (my uncle) for sharing their love and insights.

Long ago, when I first began to free-lance, Roger Swain of *Horticulture* magazine encouraged me to continue writing. He's been a friend, mentor, and a bastion of ideas ever since, and in so many ways, this book owes its birth to Roger. As the idea for this book evolved and took on a life of its own, it was nurtured by Tom Cooper, Tom Fischer (whose editing is truly masterful), Debbie Starr and Tina Schwinder at *Horticulture,* as well as Rebecca Atwater at Prentice Hall. And this volume would never have come about if Suzie and Carter Bales had not introduced me to Rebecca.

If this book is pleasant to behold, we can thank Bill Stites whose ingenious photography gave life to the words. I would also like to thank Sarah Bohorquez, Geoffrey Martin, and Will Perkins who did styling. And a debt of gratitude is owed to Trudy Bancroft, Susan Burns, the Chaplins, the Cummingses, and the Inn at Gwen Careg who lent us their windows.

But there would be no book at all without plants. I would like to thank all my coworkers—the entire Logee's Greenhouse staff—all those people who watered and trained plants, fixed furnaces, mixed soil, and answered phones while this book was being written. They are Donna Ayers-LaPointe, Lee Achten, Ann Beltrami, Carl Bisson, Sarah Bohorquez, Nina Burelle, Linda Cushman, Sharon Davis, Missy Desrochers, Karen Fafard, Rob Girard, Brenda Jacobs, Debbie Lavoie, Byron Martin, Dawn Read, Chuck Renaud, Karen Schmidt, Holly Shaw, and especially Russell Smith. I would also like to thank my friend Jack Henning—we like to think of him as a Logee's "staff member-at-large."

CONTENTS

Let There Be Light

I work in a family-run houseplant nursery. Every day, customers march through the door, amble down the steps, and snatch up the first pretty plant they encounter to bring home and put on their windowsill. I always wonder: Have they considered the light preferences of the botanical they've chosen? Will the little plant they've selected survive in their western window? Can it tolerate the bright light on their southern sill? Of course, I'm too polite to interrogate them. I wouldn't dare ask if they plan to give their newly adopted botanical roommate a proper home. But really, it's not the color of your thumb (green or otherwise) that dictates the fate of your resident botanicals. When it comes to houseplants, light is the deciding factor.

If you want to succeed with houseplants, select your plant on the basis of its light requirements rather than whether or not it tugs at your heartstrings or matches the upholstery. It's always a nasty surprise to discover that an adorable little plant demands a southern sill when you have only west-facing windows. It would be equally disconcerting to find that the ravishing bright blue bloomer you chose to contrast with the north-facing living room's cheerful yellow decor will never bear blossoms. You can crank up the thermostat to please your plants. You can water more or less often to cater to their whims. You can install humidifiers to moisten the atmosphere. But you cannot alter the orientation of your home.

So, before embarking on any plant-collecting spree, your first task is to take stock of your windowsills and their bearings. There's no need to get out the compass—just glance out the window on a sunny morning. The sun rises in the east, of course, and sets in the west. You can figure the rest out accordingly.

Our house in on North Street, a little avenue that runs east and west along the northern border of town. It's a remarkably straight

A windowseat is valuable for more than just gazing through the panes on rainy days. Here it provides a shelf to hold Begonia *'Sophie Cecile' (far left) and* Streptocarpus Constant Nymph *'Cobalt', with* Sophrolaeliacattleya Rocket Darst HCC/AOS × Deep Enamel *above and* Begonia *'Dierna' below. To the right on the windowseat* Trachelospermum asiaticum *sits beside* Begonia *'Looking Glass' (below).*

little street, and our home squarely faces the road. Therefore, we have a nice supply of windows, with direct northern, southern, eastern, and western exposures. Their exact orientation certainly simplified the research for this book. But not all roads are so precisely laid according to the compass, and not all homes are equally square on their plot. Many houses have windows that face northeast or southwest. If that's the case with your home, consider yourself lucky indeed. You can garner the western rays when the sun has moved beyond its midday position. You can bolster the botanicals in your northern windows with some early eastern sunbeams. Windows that are slightly askew compasswise provide the best of both worlds. If you are the proud owner of such sills, you can safely mingle plants from more than one section of this book.

There are other circumstances that might affect the straightforward use of this volume. When you're taking stock of your windows and their view, check for porches, overhangs, shade trees, close-set buildings, and anything else that might stand between your windowsill and the sun's rays. Generally speaking, a minor obstruction will downgrade your exposure by one step. In other words, if you've got a dead-on south window with a porch overhang, you should turn to the "East" section of this book to find appropriate plants. If you've got a west window heavily shaded by evergreens, choose plants from the "North" section of this book. And if you've got a north window blocked by a high-rise apartment next door, that exposure probably can't support plant life at all unless you boost your light level with fluorescent bulbs.

The surrounding environment can also improve exposures, allowing you to choose plants that would normally prefer to grow in a brighter situation. If you live on the upper floor of a high-rise apartment with spacious windows and no obstructing buildings close by, your eastern exposure probably receives as much light as a bright southern sill. If you live near the shore or on a lake, the water will reflect the sun's rays, adding to the available light streaming through your windows and upgrading them at least one step. North will be west, west will be east, and east will be south for all intents and purposes. By the same token, if your fenestration already faces south and it receives a superabundance of glaring light, you might need to mute the sunrays with a shade, especially in midsummer. But in most cases, you can safely let the sun shine in.

Which brings me to another point. When sun streams through

panes of glass, it is never as bright as the unfiltered sunlight available outdoors. Unless plants are actually touching panes of glass, they rarely (if ever) get sunburned when they're grown in the recommended exposure. A plant mentioned in the "South" section of this book shouldn't suffer from the full brunt of sunbeams rushing through a south-facing window. There are exceptions, of course. If you live in Arizona, you'll probably want to buffer the brutal sunlight for your own comfort as well as the health and welfare of your plants. But in most regions of the country, unfiltered sun shouldn't harm your houseplants—as long as you select plants carefully according to their light preferences.

Needless to say, you have to exercise good judgment. You can't take a plant that's been growing in very low light and suddenly plunk it onto an incredibly sunny sill. You have to increase light gradually. Actually, there's one time of year when nature works against you in this matter. In autumn, when leaves suddenly come showering down, houseplants will be inundated by bright sun. Eventually they'll appreciate the increased light, but they should be pulled away from the panes for a week or so while they adjust. The same holds true if your neighbor suddenly removes a tree or if the city decides to demolish the skyscraper next door. Plants don't like sudden changes.

As you're wandering through this book, keep in mind that I haven't mentioned all the houseplants available. Instead, I've discussed plants that I find intriguing. I highly recommend all of the plants mentioned herein. The bloomers should perform their feats without undue fuss; the foliage plants shouldn't prove peevish.

Finally, this is a book of ideas. It not only addresses the proper care and illumination of houseplants but also talks about their liberation: Houseplants have been the underdogs of horticulture. For some reason, gardeners just don't exercise the same creativity when dealing with plants indoors. This book will help you design a window garden featuring the subtle color combinations and design techniques that you employ in your garden outdoors. I hope it will move window gardening beyond the soldier-straight rows of tacky little plastic pots so pervasive at present. I hope someday houseplants will be trained, snipped, and fussed over with the same care that people lavish on their lawns. There's no reason why windows can't be cleverly designed and carefully groomed. And I hope that growers will begin to ferret out rare houseplants just as they seek sophisticated perennials for their backyards. Well-clad windowsills are what this book is all about.

Introduction

The proper place to begin this book is certainly on the south side of the house, where the sun rays are brightest. In our home, the south windows are hot spots, so to speak. At most times of the year, you'll find a couple of cats sound asleep in the warm rays of the kitchen's southerly sill, while upstairs, we often catnap in a south-facing sunporch. However, there really isn't much room for snoozing due south, because the south-facing windows are where many flowering plants must dwell.

Generally, of all the windows in the house, those that face south enjoy the most hours of sun per day, especially in the summer. In fact, at that time of year, the sun rays streaming through a south-facing window might seem brutally bright to us, the heat capable of roasting a tender tropical. And, in California, Arizona, or the warmer parts of the Midwest, it might prove necessary to filter the solar influx at high noon by pulling a curtain or adjusting a shade. But in most areas, if you don't mind the heat of the summer sun, the plants certainly won't object. The bulk of the plants mentioned in this section can take the brunt of those sunbeams and put the solar power to good use. However, you might want to move plants closer to the panes in winter and further back in midsummer. And be wary of imperfections in the glass: Old panes often have swirls and waves that can act as magnifiers and burn foliage.

Sun-worshiping plants don't like to have their solar rations cut. Although many plants that will grow in an east-, west-, or even north-facing window wouldn't mind being upgraded to a south window, most of the inhabitants of the south sill begin to deteriorate rapidly in lower-light situations.

If you're not sure of a plant's light requirements, how do you know

Many rooms enjoy the benefit of several exposures. On the east side of this room sit (from left to right) Columnea *'Yellow Dragon' and* Passiflora *'Jeannette'. On the south side of the scene are (from left to right)* Bougainvillea harrisii *'Variegata',* Hibiscus *'Janice' (on the table),* Mandevilla sanderi *(on the floor), and a windowbox containing* Pentas *'California Pink' and* Abutilon *'Moonchimes' (far right).*

if it demands a southern exposure? One symptom of stress is when new growth bends toward the window. Another is if the stems begin to stretch between leaves. Finally, the plant will begin to look ragged—leaves might drop or turn brown at the tips. Of course, it's best to keep an eye peeled for the subtle botanical body language of swaying stems that are begging for more light.

Fortunately, there is no need to worry about the daytime temperature in a south-facing window at any time of year. The sun tends to keep things fairly toasty. However, that heat can also work against you. In early spring, for example, it can send a plant into a rush of spindly growth. The remedy is to offset the daytime warmth with a ten- to fifteen-degree drop in temperature at night. This trick prevents rank growth and ensures that flowers will sit atop nice compact stems.

Flowers are what south-facing windows are all about. On southerly sills, there's ample opportunity to practice design skills as you juggle their floriferous inhabitants. You might match the interior decor with a blend of sympathetic hues. Or you can work out color patterns to give the feeling of an actual garden indoors. In our home, we're plant collectors, so our southerly windows tend to be packed with a brood of wonderful rarities and favorite sun-lovers. To mute the clamor of color, we slip in herbs kept close by both for culinary purposes and for their handsome green and silver foliage.

Abutilons

A gardener built our house. Numerous doorways allow convenient access to The Great Outdoors from all sides, and several windows catch the sun's rays from each exposure. Plants of all descriptions have come and gone from the windowsills of our house, but, for as long as anyone can remember, Grandpa Logee always grew an abutilon in the south-facing parlor window to bask in the sunbeams and blossom its little heart out.

Quite fittingly, abutilons are known as flowering maples or parlor

Boasting both ornamental leaves and plentiful flowers, Abutilon 'Clementine Variegated' *sits on a south sill.*

The trend in parlor maples is toward compact growth and plentiful blooms, as exemplified by Abutilon *'Snowfall'.*

maples, nicknames that date back to Grandpa Logee's day and refer to the plant's continual floral performance, traditional place of residence, and distinctly maple-shaped foliage. No doubt about it—without flowers, abutilons bear an uncanny resemblance to maples. But an abutilon bereft of blossoms is an infrequent vision, and the flowers reveal the plant's affiliation to the mallow family (Malvaceae). Abutilons provide the best of both worlds. The foliage is head and shoulders above the typical mallow fare, and the bell-shaped blooms, shielding their nest of fluffy yellow stamens, are much handsomer than anything you might find on a bonafide *Acer*.

The name abutilon comes from the Arabic *awbūtīlūn*, coined by the Islamic physician and philosopher Avicenna (Ibn Sīnā) who died in 1037. For his brilliant choice of names, the physician was honored with a rather unpopular species, *Abutilon avicennae* (later renamed *A. theophrasti*), a common weed that has been cursed by every farmer who ever planted a crop of cotton. There was never any doubt that abutilons belonged in the mallow family, but botanists waged a running argument as to whether abutilons were a genus unto themselves or merely a species of the genus *Sida*. Finally, the distinction between the two was established literally on the basis of shreds of evidence. In the 1820s, a botanist by the name of H. Link carried wallet-sized herbarium sheets throughout Europe from expert to expert until he won the abutilon its designation as a separate genus.

Although Grandpa Logee was undoubtedly a maverick in many ways, he was apparently not alone in his choice of parlor companions. Flowering maples were something of a fad in the late nineteenth century, when the idea of harboring anything arboreal in the parlor had a definite appeal. Parlor maples were so popular, in fact, that in 1892, when Grandpa Logee inherited his first greenhouse from a distant relative, it came equipped with a jasmine and an abutilon.

Grandpa Logee and his sons hadn't quite mastered the fine art of furnaces, so the greenhouse froze during its first winter, but the abutilon survived, which brings us to another valuable virtue that abutilons boast: They can endure the chilliest temperatures possible indoors. Flowering maples will persevere on the windowsill no matter how low you set your thermostat. And you don't need to worry when the temperatures soar in summer; abutilons won't scorch, either.

Abutilons demand several hours of direct sunrays daily. Given ample sun streaming through the glass, a parlor maple will perform with scarcely a pause throughout the year, producing dozens of sizable blossoms. On the other hand, when supplied with inadequate light, your flowering maple will stubbornly fail to flower, and it will stretch into a gangly stemmed shrub. For a balanced display of both tightly held foliage and symmetrically set blooms, rotate your plant half a turn each week so that all sides enjoy an equal dosage of light.

Abutilon flowers are prolific and colorful. A broad palette of petal colors is not uncommon in the mallow family; for example, consider the varied shades available in hibiscus and hollyhocks. Although abutilons haven't ventured into the blue spectrum yet (with the exception of the large shrubby species *A. ochsenii* and *A. vitifolium*, grown out of doors in mild climates), they portray just about every other hue. And yet it wasn't always so. Grandpa Logee had only a pink abutilon with darker etched veins and tightly furled petals to sit on his windowsill. His sons, sons-in-law, and grandsons collected species and bred them back and forth until they came up with good-size, open-faced, bell-shaped blossoms boasting glowing petals of yellow, tangerine, apricot, white, and all shades of pink to crimson. Other hybridizers followed suit and the group of cultivars became known collectively as *Abutilon ×hybridum*. Although the ancestry is vague, *A. ×hybridum* is presumed to stem from a complex medley of crosses between *A. darwinii*, *A. pictum*, and *A. rosaeflorum*. Most abutilons currently on the market are children of that triangle.

When flowering maple breeding was going fast and furious in the 1950s, the goal was to increase the color range and expand the bell size into a yawning two- to three-inch flower. No one thought twice about the overall stature of the plant. Somehow Grandpa Logee managed to wedge his three- to four-foot-tall abutilon onto the sill. No matter how heavily you pruned the older hybrids, they still showed three to five inches of bare stem between leaves. Nowadays, we prefer gapless, fully foliated plants that are slightly smaller in size. To answer the call, Longwood Gardens introduced *Abutilon* 'Moonchimes', with large, luminous yellow blossoms that look particularly alluring against a solid background of dense, deep-green leaves. With a little judicious pruning, 'Moonchimes' can easily remain under three feet in height, and its compact habit is perfect for training into standard form. Best of all, 'Moonchimes' blossoms despite low light—its year-round performance continues into autumn when most abutilons pause. We took the line one step further and introduced 'Clementine', which combines valentine red blossoms with the compact stature and unfailing floriferousness of 'Moonchimes'.

There are other abutilons available. Although several hybrids boast foliage that may be streaked or splattered with gold or silver, the salmon-blooming *A. pictum* 'Thompsonii' is the best of the bunch. In fact, it is among the few abutilons featuring both variegated leaves and prolific blossoms. Like Grandpa Logee's old-fashioned pink abutilon, 'Thompsonii' has tightly furled petals, but the blooms compensate for their scaled-down size with unabashed floriferousness. A close runner-up would be *A. megapotamicum* 'Variegata', called the Chinese lantern for its dangling yellow blossoms peeking from long red calyxes. The Chinese lantern is a sprawling plant with long chains of triangular, deep-green leaves enhanced by a checkerboard of gold. It makes a handsome hanging plant in a bright southern exposure but can easily look like hell if deprived of maximum sun. 'Marianne' is a variation on the Chinese lantern theme with comparatively lackluster dangling yellow flowers spilling from blush-colored calyxes. Like its parent *A. megapotamicum*, it needs a lot of light.

Like all members of the mallow family, abutilons are tormented by whiteflies and red spider mites, so keep a vigilant eye on their leaves and check "Houseplant Care" (page 197) for remedies. Besides that one little hitch, abutilons are trouble-free plants. To encourage blossoming, you should keep an abutilon tightly potted rather than graduating its container continually. As a result, the tip growth might wilt between waterings, but don't fret—flowering maples are forgiving plants and will perk up immediately after a drink. Don't overreact and overwater—abutilons can rot when anchored in sopping soil. Flowering maples should not be fertilized heavily. To encourage good leaf color and abundant blossoms, fertilize once a month with a balanced feed such as 20-20-20. You might stretch the intervals between feeding to once every six to eight weeks during the dark days from November to March.

Even inherently compact abutilons such as 'Moonchimes' and 'Clementine' require pruning to encourage a plump, full plant. I urge you to start early. Why let your plant run up into an undisciplined, naked-kneed eyesore just for the sake of a few immediate buds? Begin pinching when the plant is less than a foot tall and continue wielding the pruning shears throughout its career. The reward will be a bounty of bell-shaped blooms worthy of a prime spot on the parlor windowsill.

Acalyphas

Not everyone likes acalyphas. The very young and the young at heart find them totally beguiling. More prim and proper indoor gardeners do not approve. Envision foot-long, shocking-pink streamers resembling red-hot cattails or oversize fuzzy caterpillars dancing in every breeze and you've drawn a fairly accurate picture of acalyphas in full regalia. To some eyes, the blossoms bear a resemblance to flocked fabrics, thus earning *Acalypha hispida* its nickname—the chenille plant. They look like something Walt Disney might dream up, but Mother Nature beat him to it.

Acalyphas are tactile plants. Kids can never resist petting them and adults occasionally indulge in a surreptitious stroke or two when no one's looking. Acalyphas add a little levity to your windows and give you something to do with your hands besides weeding and pruning. Personally, I'm rather fond of these lighthearted, therapeutic plants.

Acalypha hispida, from New Guinea, is the most popular member of the family. Without its chenilles, *A. hispida* would look boring indeed—like a poinsettia before its floral bracts color up. In fact, acalyphas, along with poinsettias, belong to the spurge family, or Euphorbiaceae. But unlike poinsettias, acalyphas don't confine their performance to a single season. In a sunny window, *A. hispida* will always have a crop of fuzzies dangling about.

Whether you love or hate *A. hispida* has a lot to do with how it's grown. A single stretching stem punctuated by a few plump but awkward danglers can look rather wacky, whereas a densely foliated, frequently pruned chenille plant accented by abundant blossoms has a touch of class. Sort of. Since acalyphas never pause in their performance, pruning can be done at any time of year. Our secret trick is to rotate acalyphas. We don't hesitate to give a plant its annual shearing because a stand-in is waiting to be hustled to the fore. Moreover, we're not shy about snipping the plant to a stubble. Acalyphas initiate new growth from old wood at a moment's notice. Even after a close shave, in two to three months the plant will look better than ever, with a dense crop of foliage and flowers.

Several other acalyphas do variations on the furry-flowered theme. If you disapprove of *A. hispida*'s shocking pink-and-green color combination, try the clone 'Alba'. 'Alba' is nearly identical to the common chenille, except its catkins are longer, fluffier, and a sedate creamy

---

Where windows line a wall, the room can become a conservatory. This window hosts (left to right) a jade plant, Crassula ovata *(formerly* C. argentea), *a tall standard-in-training of* Acalypha hispida, *the zonal pelargonium 'Rococo', the scented pelargonium 'Logeei',* Bougainvillea *'Texas Dawn', and* Clerodendrum thomsoniae.

white shade instead of blush pink. Then there's *A. repens*, a sprawling version that has recently gained publicity and popularity under the nickname of strawberry firetails. The fame is well deserved. Since strawberry firetails is self-branching, it achieves instant drama the moment you nestle a few plants together in a hanging basket. The firetails are about as long and thick as your thumb and they pop out all over. This is an intensely rewarding plant, especially popular with junior gardeners who might even remember to apply water when they're petting the firetails.

Not all acalyphas have prominent catkins. Long before *A. hispida* came into cultivation, Victorians were oohing and aahing over *A. wilkesiana* (formerly called *A. tricolor*), brought from the Pacific Islands in 1866. Although it bears only sparsely tufted flower stalks, the foliage needs no further adornment. Known as the copperleaf, *A. wilkesiana* has broad, closely stacked, brilliant copper leaves mottled and streaked with orange. With just a little pruning, it branches broadly and stands no taller than three feet. It's quite a sight, especially standing beside *A. wilkesiana* 'Obovata', with rounder, darker leaves enhanced by orange edges, or *A. wilkesiana* 'Moorea', with undulating, crinkly leaves, or any of its other variations. If space is limited, try *A. godseffiana* 'Heterophylla', which has pencil-thin, orange, yellow, and green leaves enhanced by modest catkins. It grows slowly into a dense, two- to three-foot specimen.

All acalyphas are heavy drinkers and they'll go into a deathlike wilt if water isn't immediately forthcoming. Fortunately, it's only an act. Most acalyphas perk up as soon as the watering can arrives. The only exception is *A. repens*, which isn't bluffing—its leaf edges will turn brown following a serious swoon.

You can hardly dissuade an acalypha from blooming. But lack of light will discourage the flowers and overenthusiastic feeding can also call a halt to the performance. Like a geranium, the branches bend toward a light source, so keep turning the plant to bathe its entire circumference in sun. Temperature is not usually a problem. Most acalyphas grow lush in cool as well as warm environments, with the

One of the most dramatic windowsill denizens is the chenille plant, Acalypha hispida, *also known as red-hot cattails. In the distance are the buttery blossoms of* Allamanda cathartica *'Williamsii'.*

exception of *A. godseffiana* 'Heterophylla', which drops leaves if the thermometer frequently drops below 60 degrees Fahrenheit. And acalyphas will good-naturedly endure low humidity if necessary.

In addition to pruning, grooming is important for acalyphas. The chenilles turn brown after a week or so and eventually fall to the ground, but a little sprucing once a week will keep the plant tidy. Because the spent chenilles come off in your hand, no pruners are necessary.

Although acalyphas are delightfully easy to grow, they have one drawback: Whiteflies and red spider mites find them intriguing. Keep an eye peeled for the first sign of trouble, and use the appropriate remedy if it appears. It's a small price to pay for a plant that provides a hint of horticultural humor in an otherwise serious business.

Allamandas

Not every windowsill can accommodate an allamanda. Allamandas are hefty, oversize plants that monopolize a lion's share of the sill. And yet they also put on a big show: Imagine golden trumpets the size of tea saucers dangling by the dozen from a rigid-stemmed vine richly clad in whorls of six-inch-long leaves. If you have a roomy window, an allamanda will fill the expanse hastily. Or, if you prefer to feature a soloist rather than stuffing a smaller sill with a botanical choir, an allamanda makes a loud statement a cappella.

Until quite recently, we knew only one allamanda—*Allamanda cathartica* 'Williamsii', and it's still the best of the lot. 'Williamsii' is often called the golden trumpet, a common name that refers to the vine's most compelling attribute. The golden trumpet's gangly branches and its awkward whorls of foliage are definitely not the traits that immediately catch your eye. With allamandas, flowers are the thing. Those blossoms are memorable, and they compensate for all the allamanda's less savory qualities. Throughout the year, brilliant four-inch-wide trumpets gape in clusters from the twiggy branches. Not only are those blooms an eye-riveting shade of sunflower yellow, but each deep throat is streaked with blush red, adding definition and punctuating the target point for the benefit of potential pollinators. With good light, those all-important flowers will put on an unceasing performance throughout the year. In its native South America, *A.*

A newcomer to the scene is the velvet-petaled Allamanda 'Chocolate Cherry'.

cathartica is an energetic vine that climbs by leaning on sturdier neighbors. The species has a rather limp growth habit and relatively small butter-yellow blooms (small being two to three inches as opposed to the three- to four-inch petal span of 'Williamsii'), each accented by a white throat. But it's nearly impossible to find the plain *A. cathartica* on the market nowadays. Apparently, 'Williamsii' has stolen all the species' thunder.

And truth to tell, 'Williamsii' is quite an improvement. In addition to bearing larger, showier, and more numerous flowers than its parent, 'Williamsii' features a self-supporting growth habit compared to the rather limp appendages of the species, although it is not much denser than its parent. The plump stems are loosely clad in whorls of

The handsome pollen streaks marking the throat of Allamanda catharctica *'Williamsii' have evolved to guide insects toward the center of the night-scented yellow trumpets.*

three to four long slender leaves. No matter how much light you give the vine (and allamandas demand a lot of light), there's a gap of at least four inches between leaf whorls. Early pruning will encourage side growth, but you're always battling the plant's inherent urge to stretch. In our greenhouse, we let the grandfather of all our golden trumpets amble helter-skelter overhead, providing shade for a potting bench beneath. When the days begin to shorten, we cut it back drastically to allow the winter sun to stream in. For a few months, we see only a smattering of blossoms until spring brings a flush of new growth and a fresh crop of buds. By the middle of May, the vine is going full tilt with bushels of blooms, each emitting a wonderful evening aroma for all the world like Manischewitz wine. During the day, the blossoms of *A. c.* 'Williamsii' have no scent whatsoever.

Recently, a double form of *A. cathartica* called 'Flore Plena' came back into cultivation. Originally discovered in Florida in the 1950s, the bright-yellow double buds feature a blossom within a blossom—like the old hose-in-hose primroses. To tell the truth, they look more like an aberration than a thing of beauty. But the vine of *A. c.* 'Flore Plena' is more compact than any other allamanda and those contorted blossoms open in even greater profusion than the prolific 'Williamsii'. The real draw, however, is the fragrance. 'Flore Plena' emits the delicious aroma of sugarcoated candy, and the scent floats forth seductively both night and day.

There are other allamandas around as well. *Allamanda cathartica* 'Hendersonii', named for the nineteenth-century nurseryman who first introduced the vine, is a rather watered-down version of the *cathartica* theme. Not only are the branches straggly, with embarrassing six-inch gaps covered by no leaves at all, but the flowers are a sort of sad off-cream color with brick-tinted overlays. In Victorian times, when all sorts of drab things were the rage, 'Hendersonii' was given a hero's welcome and won fame and fortune under the common name of brown bud, which gives you some idea of the coloration. *Allamanda cathartica* 'Chocolate Cherry' is a recent improvement on 'Hendersonii', with velvety maroon flowers sprouting from branches that are slightly gangly, but certainly not as awkward as the appendages of its parent.

Allamandas must reach a certain size before they acquire any sort of grace. At first they are all groping arms and legs flailing out in every direction. But with a few strategic snips of the pruning shears and some tactical manipulation, an allamanda can easily be disciplined into shape. Timing is the key—it's essential to begin training early in the plant's career. Fortunately, allamandas sprout side shoots from every whorl of leaves below the pinching point. Still, the best time to start is when the allamanda has only two or three whorls. Pinch the top and you'll have the branches necessary to provide a strong base.

The obvious exception here is when the plant is targeted to become a straight-stemmed standard. Despite its size, 'Williamsii' makes a handsome, quick, and easy standard with a strong stem topped by an informally loose crown. You will need a sturdy support to shoulder the allamanda's bulk. At first, a strong bamboo stake will suffice. Later, when your allamanda graduates into an eight-inch pot, you might want to invest in a wooden trellis anchored in the pot's soil. An allamanda's branches are brittle at maturity, but they can be bent into a wide arch when they are still young and tender. Prune awkward branches in winter when the blossom display is pausing anyway, but keep in mind that buds appear on the tips of branches. In spring, there will be a flush of new growth followed by a crop of plump buds.

Temperatures are also a pressing issue for allamandas. Although they will reputedly endure a touch of frost when planted outdoors in the South, allamandas don't look hale and hearty indoors unless you keep the thermometer above 60 degrees Fahrenheit at night, which is a tad warm for many economy-conscious homeowners. Chlorosis (a yellowing of the leaves) is the first symptom of a chill—you can fertilize an allamanda till you're blue in the face and it won't utilize iron when temperatures dip consistently below 60 degrees.

Watering can be tricky. Indoor gardeners tend to water more heavily in the winter (when houseplants have a captive audience, they tend to receive a superfluity of tender loving care), and winter is the worst time to overwater an allamanda. Let the vine dry out to the point of slight wilting before applying water again. In spring, when new growth begins, the vine will dry out more frequently.

Allamandas are hungry plants. Rather than adopting a rigid fertilizing schedule, we use the foliar color as a barometer to tell us when to feed. Allamandas should be deep green. If the leaves begin to pale, turn yellow, or become mottled rather than solid in hue, it's time to fertilize. In spring and summer, allamandas should be fed every three to four weeks with 20-20-20 or any balanced feed.

By the same token, allamandas demand frequent repotting into a very beefy soil. I've seen allamandas grown in soilless mixes, but they look very sad indeed. Allamandas require the real thing (composted manure, that is, rather than chemical fertilizer) underfoot. And we always anchor our allamandas in clay containers—they tend to topple in plastic.

Allamandas might not be the easiest plants in the world to entertain, but they make satisfying roommates. If you need companionship after a long day's work, there's nothing like a fulsome allamanda blaring its golden trumpets and sending its fragrance floating on the evening air.

Bougainvilleas

Deep inside, most folks yearn for a bougainvillea on their window-sill. Who wouldn't love to host a pot or two of those graceful flowering vines wending their way between the window panes? And yet you won't find a bougainvillea peering from every house in town. Far from it. Bougainvilleas, it seems, are usually admired from afar.

This is because bougainvilleas have traditionally been regarded with a mixture of fear and trembling. As far as I can see, though, the vine has done nothing to deserve the prevailing paranoia. The plant's sole fault is its frail appearance—bougainvilleas exude a fragile beauty, and gardeners assume that delicate bloomers must be difficult. Thus bougainvilleas are held at arm's length and their name is only mentioned in the same breath as orchids and other insurmountable challenges. For a few brave gardeners, this reputation only heightens the vine's appeal. But those willing to venture into bougainvilleas quickly discover that the fragile beauty is a façade. Bougainvilleas don't need a greenhouse or exceptionally high humidity. In fact, bougainvilleas will happily meander and produce blossoms galore on the average sunny windowsill.

Even if bougainvilleas weren't eyed as forbidden fruit, they would be attractive. Native to South America, this member of the four-o'clock family, or Nyctaginaceae, is a twining, thick-stemmed vine with intermittent forest-green leaves tipped by clusters of blooms. Bougainvilleas possess an inherent poetry. The vines swoop and arch, forming the most seductive curves in horticulture. Their graceful branches are forever laden with crisp umbels of papery flower bracts that come in the most fascinating nuances of hue and yet change like chameleons to reflect captured sunrays.

Actually, it's not the blossoms themselves that make a bougainvillea memorable. In fact, the long, oboe-shaped bougainvillea flowers are hardly worth a second glance. It's the bracts shielding those flowers that have won the vine both fame and fortune. The bracts, which cluster in plump bunches like hydrangeas, are tissue-paper thin, intricately textured, and come in every shade from subtle pink to burning magenta. Their colors are fascinatingly unstable, altering with the changing light. In fact, at first glance, bougainvilleas are often mistaken for sweet peas—both have a certain luminous splendor.

You will see neither blossoms nor bracts on your bougainvillea if you don't have a sunny window. When bougainvilleas were first introduced into Britain in the mid-1800s, the vine was abandoned as worthless because it refused to blossom in Britain's overcast climate. In sunnier France, bougainvilleas revealed their true qualities; they were popularized and named for the French explorer who circumnavigated the globe in the 1760s, Louis Antoine de Bougainville.

The bougainvilleas that bask in our sunny windowsills are actually a far cry from the original species. Most cultivars are the convoluted mixture of three species—*Bougainvillea glabra*, *B. peruviana*, and *B. spectabilis*. Early in the bougainvillea's history, the purplish magenta 'Crimson Lake' and its twin sister, 'Mrs. Butt', made such a smash hit that they won their own pseudo-botanical designation, *Bougainvillea ×buttiana*. For some reason, in southwest landscape plantings, bougainvilleas begin and end with 'Crimson Lake'—you'll rarely see another color climbing around outdoors. But this monotony cannot be blamed on a lack of alternatives. We have pinks (we call our luminous heirloom pink 'Texas Dawn'), oranges (one particularly impressive pumpkin-colored hybrid is 'Camarillo Fiesta' with huge bracts that put on their strongest show in autumn and winter), salmon, yellow, and lilac as well as magenta. There are double varieties featuring a nest of multicolored bracts as well as the single varieties. And yet, in my opinion, all the different shades cannot compare with the pearly white cultivar, 'Snow White', so densely packed with large bracts that the vine is scarcely visible when the flowers are in full tilt.

Perhaps one reason for the supremacy of 'Crimson Lake' is its cold tolerance. 'Crimson Lake' will endure a nip of frost now and then, but it sheds leaves, flowers, and bracts immediately after a chill and the foliage isn't fast to return. Flowers follow even more lethargically. If it's midwinter flowers that you want on your windowsill, you'll need to keep the temperature moderate. The thermometer should remain above 63 degrees Fahrenheit both night and day. When a bougainvillea is slightly chilly, its leaves blush pink in protest. The flush

—

A south-facing sliding door is the perfect place for a catnap in midwinter. Also basking in the sun are a pair of Myrtus communis *'Microphylla' columns flanking a wreath of* Bougainvillea harrisii *'Variegata'. Close by is an herb wreath woven by Joy Logee Martin.*

In autumn and winter, Bougainvillea *'Orange Fiesta' forms huge clusters of glowing floral bracts.*

looks lovely, but it foretells more drastic acts of defiance in the future. If the inclement climate continues, new growth will be small and sickle-shaped until one fine day when everything will dramatically drop. It's not a pretty sight.

High temperatures are all well and good but when the room is warm, the atmosphere tends to dry out. Lack of humidity will cause bougainvilleas to react with the same histrionics employed to signal their distaste for chilly conditions: The leaves will crinkle and drop. They absolutely hate shafts of hot air blowing through their foliage and the nearby output of air conditioners is equally disdained. Keep the humidity above 40 percent by means of a pebble tray, pans of evaporating water set beside heat sources, or a humidifier.

Light is the most important factor for producing flowers, but there is another trick to encouraging blossoms on a bougainvillea. We let our vines wilt slightly before we water again. It isn't hard to do—bougainvilleas wilt with alarming frequency. Don't let them keel over completely, but wait until the tips nod before quenching their thirst again—buds will then form even on shy-blooming cultivars.

Rather than pruning bougainvilleas, we wind them around sturdy stakes and sizable trellises. The stems are brittle, so make wide curves. A simple wreath form is easiest—just wind the stem in circles. If you are struck by the urge to prune, remember that blossoms are produced on new growth. If these flowering tips are removed, you will sacrifice a year's blossoms. Prune only roving, whiplike growth that is at odds with your weaving scheme.

The stem is not the only brittle part of a bougainvillea; the roots are also brittle, and can be detached from their stem by the slightest disturbance. You'll know immediately if it happens—the foliage will wilt pathetically and watering will not bolster its spirits. Since the situation is irreparable, repot gently and try not to wiggle the stem while you're at it. When promotions become necessary, use a beefy, rich soil that is heavy enough to anchor the broad, woody stem.

Bougainvilleas are usually expensive because the vine can only be propagated from old wood. The rooting process takes several months, during which time a mist system and bottom heat are continually required. It's not the sort of feat that an amateur can undertake successfully.

Bougainvilleas are not bothered by many pests, but mealy bugs find them attractive. When you're combating the pest (see ''Houseplant Care,'' page 197, for the specifics), be sure to penetrate the dense foliar mass. Bougainvilleas are fraught with hidden nooks and crannies, but that's part of their charm.

Bougainvilleas have one trait that some fastidious gardeners find bothersome: The bracts flutter to the vine's feet when they are finished. I rather like this confetti effect. However, if you'd rather not sweep up after your botanical roommates, choose a double-flowering bougainvillea—the blossoms will dry right on the stem until they're removed. Either dried or fresh, double bougainvilleas linger like hydrangeas in bouquets.

Clerodendrums

Gardeners may claim that they prefer the quiet things in life, but a quick peek at their windowsills reveals a deep-rooted desire for drama. Let's face it—when given a choice between shy and showy, gardeners go for the buxom bloomers and knock-'em-dead colors every time. Deep inside, we're all party animals, and that's the crux of the clerodendrums' broad appeal.

I go with the crowd when it comes to clerodendrums. They open in some of the snappiest shades you'll ever lay eyes upon. They do so willingly and without undue fuss. And best of all, clerodendrums bloom in seasons when flowers are sparse. In autumn, for example, just when you desperately need blossoms and there's scarcely another flower in sight, *Clerodendrum wallichii* and *C. splendens* burst forth in lush abandon. In early spring when you're famished for flowers, *C. speciosissimum* starts blooming long before the rest of the crowd kicks in.

Of the four hundred clerodendrums on this planet, only half a dozen are commonly grown. And of that handful, *Clerodendrum thomsoniae* definitely wins the popularity poll. *C. thomsoniae* is commonly called the glory vine or glory bower, which gives you some hint of the entertainment in store. It's a rambunctious, sturdy-stemmed climber with large, handsome, deeply veined leaves enhanced throughout three seasons by some of the world's least subtle flowers. The blossoms resemble oversize bleeding hearts (another of the plant's nicknames is bleeding heart vine) and their prolonged moment of glory begins in spring when dense clusters of pure white pouches (technically calyxes) start to inflate. When the pouch has reached a nice degree of roundness, half-inch-wide, blood-red blossoms slowly emerge, accented by jutting stamens. The calyxes cling long after the red bloom has withered; gradually, they turn paper thin and blush burgundy before setting berries. The berries sprout readily when planted, providing little glory bowers for envious friends and relatives.

A southern windowsill nurtures (left to right) Allamanda cathartica *'Williamsii',* Clerodendrum thomsoniae, Pentas *'California Lavender',* Clerodendrum ugandense, *and* Bougainvillea *'Raspberry Ice' (foreground).*

Even a fledgling will produce a few clusters of cheerful flowers throughout spring, summer, and early autumn. Mature vines, wound to a three-foot frame, are smothered in blossoms—you can scarcely see the leaves beneath their red and white bounty.

Native to West Africa, *C. thomsoniae* was named for W. C. Thomson, a missionary who sent the vine to Edinburgh in 1861. In Britain, Thomson's namesake was given a hero's welcome and hustled into the nearest primitive greenhouse where it was alternately baked or chilled by fickle furnaces. The fact that *C. thomsoniae* survived the ordeal provides a clue to the vine's iron constitution. Although the glory bower will tolerate chilly temperatures, it will slip into dormancy and drop its leaves. In fact, *C. thomsoniae* prefers toasty conditions—temperatures that dip no lower than 65 degrees Fahrenheit at night, with a 10- to 15-degree hike during the day.

There are other spin-offs on the *C. thomsoniae* theme. There's a variegated version with very handsome cream-marbled leaves but infrequent flowers. There's also a hybrid between *C. thomsoniae* and *C. splendens* with magenta rather than white calyxes, but the monochromatic flowers only appear in autumn. Neither of these plants can touch *C. thomsoniae*'s glory.

Although it is hard to surpass this superstar's splendor, several other species are worth a look. If you can forgive *C. speciosissimum*'s cumbersome name, this bush-type clerodendrum is a perfect candidate for indoors. *Clerodendrum speciosissimum* (someone's got to find a nickname for this plant) does best in a southern exposure, but will also grow and blossom in an east or west window. The leaves are felted and heart-shaped, but the foliage isn't the main draw. The clincher is the scarlet blossoms, which first appear when the plant is scarcely a foot tall. As with most clerodendrums, the performance is prolonged. In this case, the flowers start as a little medallion of color tucked between the plush leaves and slowly elongate into a candelabrum of long-lasting color continuing through most of the year. In a pot, the plant remains a compact two to three feet; in its native Java, however, it towers ten feet above the undergrowth. *Clerodendrum speciosissimum* is easy to grow, especially from seed, which is pro-

Clerodendrum thomsoniae *bears an impressive abundance of red blossoms peeking from creamy white bracts.*

duced abundantly. But it has one fault. A harmless, naturally occurring but nonetheless disquieting grayish exudate often forms on the undersides of the leaves, which makes them look a little dingy. Unfortunately, there isn't a thing you can do to prevent or remove it.

Year-round bloomers may be the mainstay of the windowsill, but seasonal performers add a little anticipation to the scene. In my opinion, autumn wouldn't be bearable without *C. splendens* and *C. wallichii*. When the windowsill is stuck in a dreary lull, these two bloomers come rushing to your aid. My favorite is *C. wallichii*, with its long, wisterialike chains of creamy blossoms. The gracefully arched stems are clad with slender foliage, and the plant usually stands two to three feet tall, with a foot or so of stem hidden by the dangling blossoms. In addition to its timing, *C. wallichii* also boasts an easy disposition. With no encouragement whatsoever, it produces suckers from the base, expanding the plant's girth and increasing the floral display. The foliage is always a deep green even if you forget to fertilize, and insects seldom attempt to gnaw on its leather-thick leaf surface.

Although *C. wallichii* is a fairly subtle plant, its screaming scarlet cousin, *C. splendens*, is definitely not. In autumn, its three-alarm display consists of quantities of lipstick-red blossoms borne amid vigorously vining stems and glossy, almost round leaves. Contrary to its easy-to-care-for relatives, *C. splendens* requires high humidity (at least 60 percent) to prevent leaf edge browning, the brightest light possible, and warm night temperatures.

With a little imagination, you can see the family resemblance between most of the clerodendrums, but *C. ugandense* scarcely seems like part of the clan. In the blossom department, *C. ugandense* overshadows almost all its relatives with airy spires of aquamarine and cobalt-blue blooms, earning this clerodendrum the nickname of butterfly bush. The lower lip of each blossom is cobalt while four paler blue petals stand in pairs above, like wings taking flight. To complete the image, two antennaelike stamens quiver in the breeze.

Clerodendrum ugandense's flowers may be irresistible, but the hapless grower needs to know what lies below those gorgeous blue blossoms. Once the plant reaches maturity, the floral spires sit atop a few feet of lanky, nearly naked stems. Of course, you can prune the stems to encourage branching, but pruning can't be done after early spring or the blossom display will be curtailed. Since the stems turn woody and leafless in a year's time, the only remedy is to start fresh every spring with tip cuttings and discard the older gangly plant.

The search continues for windowsill-suitable clerodendrums, and just recently we found a clerodendrum that opens in the dead of winter and puts on a performance that makes its other swank cousins pale in comparison. Native to the forests of the Philippines, C. *quadri-loculare* stands only two to three feet tall with large but densely packed dark-bronze and burgundy leaves that look fetching throughout the year. In November, orbs of buds swell and slowly send out long, slender, white-and-pink-tinged flowers, shooting out like fireworks from the crown of each stem. The extravaganza goes on throughout the winter as more buds emerge. It's quite a show.

For all their charms, clerodendrums are not demanding plants. With the exception of C. *wallichii* and C. *ugandense*, most species prefer the soil to dry out between waterings. They should be fertilized every month from April through November with a balanced fertilizer, again with the exception of C. *wallichii* and C. *ugandense*, which should be fed year round. In February or March, just before your clerodendrums revive from their winter rest, give them a stern pruning to encourage branching. Then just let them grow out lush and floriferous. Tie vining types, such as C. *thomsoniae*, C. *splendens* and C. ×*speciosum* to the curtain rod, or wind them loosely around and around on a trellis for a display of even greater glory.

Geraniums

In addition to an imposing bay window in the parlor, we also have south-facing sills in the kitchen. Somehow, tropicals just don't seem at home in a room where muddied boots are lined up by the door and plant catalogs are strewn hither and yon. In fact, although we've never put it to the test, I doubt a humidity-loving tropical plant could survive so close to our well-tended and frequently fed woodstove.

In winter, some hard-working herbs sit on sills conveniently close to where dinner is prepared. In summer, the herbs are sent outside and geraniums cheerfully take up residence in the windows. The geraniums are sufficiently informal to fit with the general flow of a kitchen, their electric colors brighten the mood, and they tolerate the

inevitable jostling experienced in a room of continual comings and goings.

Actually, the plants in our windows are pelargoniums. You and I might know them as geraniums, but those bastions of street-corner window boxes were long ago reclassified. They remain in the family Geraniaceae, but they are no longer bonafide geraniums. (This also applies to the scented-leaved, ivy-leaved, and Martha Washington types.) The British meticulously call pelargoniums by their proper name, but in America we just couldn't make the switch. Everyone here still refers to them as geraniums, and I would hate to break with tradition.

To be honest, I'm not overly fond of those boisterous, bright-red geraniums splashed all over cemeteries in early summer. Among the garden-center crowd, they are known as zonal geraniums by virtue of the dark, horseshoe-shaped zone marking each leaf. I find zonal geraniums too fat, beefy, and gawky in stature for the windowsill. Moreover, their colors are generally too gaudy for my taste, and they rarely match the decor indoors. But there are some notable exceptions. Fully double types, such as the delicately colored white and whisper-pink 'Appleblossom Rosebud', chiffon pink 'Rococo', and deep red 'Rosette', are specifically bred for windowsill growing. In fact, the flowers collect water and turn to mush if the plants are grown outside.

Instead of the lanky types, our kitchen windowsills are host to a party of dwarf zonal geraniums. These lilliputian zonals are equally floriferous, nearly as easy to grow, and they have a charm that their big brothers totally lack. Dwarf geraniums have leaves no larger than an inch wide (many are fingernail size), the plants stand anywhere up to a foot tall, and the floral umbels are borne on neatly shortened stalks. The dwarfs bloom in the same broad range of hues as the zonals, but those colors look endearing when dished out in smaller doses. To top it all off, a grouping of dwarf geraniums can fit into the sort of window box that will perch comfortably on the insides of a sill.

As I hinted, dwarf geraniums aren't as easily grown as regular zonals. Since the foliage is so tightly stacked, they demand good air

In spring, pelargoniums of all types start to bloom. Shown here are (left to right) a standard of the scented pelargonium 'Lady Plymouth', the mini-regal 'Spring Park', and the ivy-leaved 'Nutmeg Lavender'.

circulation to prevent disease from settling in. In summer, our kitchen window and pantry door are always open, so there's an excellent cross-breeze. We've never had a problem. Nevertheless, it's wise to take further precautions. To be on the safe side, all geraniums should be watered in the morning of a sunny day. And when watering, try to keep the foliage dry. Other than that, you're home free. Dwarf geraniums tend to be self-branching, but a few strategic pinches will reinforce that tendency. Keep them tightly potbound and be stingy with feedings—even the smallest geranium will stretch if given too much oomph.

I replant my kitchen window box yearly, so, for diversity, some summers I fill it with ivy geraniums rather than dwarfs. As the name infers, ivy geraniums do an excellent job of looking, acting, and even smelling like ivy. But they boast one major bonus: The shiny, deep-green leaves of ivy geraniums are adorned with plentiful blossoms. Typical of the single-flowering types are the Swiss Balcony geraniums, with loose leaves and equally airy, thin-petaled blossoms in shocking pink. The semidouble bloomers are slightly tighter in their growth habit and do an even better job of impersonating English ivy. They blossom in a broad range of shades including light lavender ('La France'), dark crimson ('Royal Blood'), and creamy salmon ('Apricot Blossom'). The true doubles assume a much more compact stance, forming a curly mass of deep-green leaves adorned by dense, many-petaled blossoms just like rosebuds. So far, they are limited to shades of pink, the best being 'Sybil Holmes' and 'Beauty of Eastbourne'.

Although ivy geraniums might look like English ivy, they will not tolerate shade with the same good grace. Ivy-leaved geraniums must have bright light to bloom. They happily endure the baking sun of the Southwest; in fact, in less sun-drenched regions, they flower only during the longest days of the year. They all require pruning to achieve density, and a hanging basket will generally need three to five rooted cuttings packed solidly together. Like most other geraniums, ivy-leaved types are virtually pest free. But they do have one draw-

A southern sill with (left to right) Mandevilla sanderi *'Red Riding Hood',* Myrtus communis *'Microphylla' trained into a standard,* Pentas *'California Lavender', a globe of* Rosmarinus officinalis, *mini-regal pelargonium 'Earliana', scented pelargonium 'Orange', a standard-in-training of* Pelargonium *'Prince Rupert Variegated', and* Abutilon *'Moonchimes'.*

back—ivy geraniums are prone to a virus that causes sudden and devastating stem rot. Be sure to purchase disease-resistant stock; most of the newer hybrids have excellent resistance.

Just steps from the kitchen, there's a sinkside pantry window where we do the washing up. It's no one's favorite job, so we hang a scented-leaved geranium in the accompanying window to distract the attention of anyone elected to do the dinner dishes. Somehow, it eases the drudgery. Scented-leaved geraniums are fascinating plants. They come in a remarkable inventory of shapes and sizes, and emit an even more impressive array of mouthwatering scents. In our kitchen window, we hang one of the compact basket types—coconut (*Pelargonium parviflorum*), nutmeg (*P. fragrans*), apple (*P. odoratissimum*), or 'Logeei' (Old Spice–scented). But other scented geraniums are suitable for windowsill purposes. Most popular are the rose-scented geraniums. For a window garden, select one of the compact rose hybrids such as 'Little Gem', variegated 'Lady Plymouth', or 'Attar of Roses'. Beyond rose, there are plenty of more adventuresome varieties, including strawberry, orange, lemon, filbert, cinnamon, ginger, lime, and apricot. All of these can be pruned to remain within bounds. Avoid the giants such as peppermint, grape leaf, and 'Giant Oak'—otherwise you'll spend your days trying to thwart their tendency to take over the house.

Some scientists believe that scented-leaved geraniums evolved their fragrances to keep predators at bay. Maybe so—they're certainly rarely pestered by insects. If whiteflies are desperate, they will attack scented geraniums, but only as a last resort. Aside from occasional pruning, scented geraniums are probably the easiest plants in the world for a windowsill. And yet watering can be a delicate balance until you become accustomed to the schedule. Although scented geraniums dislike overwatering, their foliage will yellow if they are forced to go thirsty too long. After that, just follow the familiar geranium formula: tight pots, heavy soil, and hold the fertilizer.

You might find a few Martha Washington geraniums (officially, hybrids of *P. cucullatum*) here and there being sold for Valentine's or Mother's Day, but they certainly don't have the presence (or omnipresence) that other geraniums enjoy. Actually, there's a good reason: Most Martha Washington (also known as Regal) geraniums bloom only in spring and early summer before temperatures shoot up, and they blossom only following a cooling period when night temperatures plummet to 50 degrees Fahrenheit or lower. For these reasons, they're more popular in Britain than in the United States.

It's a pity, though, that Americans can't love the Martha Washingtons for their seasonal charms. After all, primroses and forced bulbs haven't suffered in popularity polls just because they make a brief appearance. Fleeting though it may be, the floral display of most Martha Washingtons far outshines other geraniums. Each blossom is at least three inches wide and there are four or five flowers to an umbel. The flowers bear an uncanny resemblance to rhododendron blossoms, although they unfold in a much broader range of shades. In fact, Martha Washingtons claim the widest spectrum in the entire genus, including lavender, peach, magenta, purple, and white with varying patterns on the upper and lower petals.

Martha Washingtons break all the geranium rules. Unlike other members of the clan, they're prone to whiteflies and mealybugs. They follow the family preference for a lean yet heavy soil, but they like plenty of root room. And though they had to share this chapter with their relations, the truth is that Martha Washingtons don't require a south-facing window—east or west will do quite nicely.

Just as endearing but equally transient are the Martha Washington offspring known as pansy geraniums. Looking for all the world like pert Johnny-jump-ups with deep-wine and royal-purple petals, they blossom for a very short stint in spring. In that same vein, the British recently began crossing Martha Washingtons with the miniature lemon-scented geranium (*P. crispum*) to yield the mini-regal or angel geraniums. These hybrids reputedly bloom longer, with flowers in a broader range of colors than the pansy types, and boast foliage with a hint of fragrance. They hold promise.

Geraniums have a long tradition on windowsills. They were among the first flowering plants to slip indoors from the garden and they've been sitting on the sill ever since. There's something wholesome about geraniums. In our kitchen, they seem like part of the family.

Herbs

Long before folks developed an appetite for fiddling with flowers inside, they dutifully dug, potted, and brought indoors plants of parsley, sage, rosemary, and thyme for the winter months. The practice was propitious, but it wasn't done for aesthetic reasons. Rather, it was a step taken from necessity. Who could survive winter without medicinal and culinary essentials close at hand? Herbs were the first houseplants, welcomed indoors because they had a service to perform.

But before you conjure up visions of robust rosemarys and plump, salubrious lavenders sitting on colonial sills begging to be plucked, bear in mind that eighteenth-century windows were not what they are today. Glass was expensive, thick, and employed very sparingly. Windows were meager or nonexistent, and the light-loving herbs that were trundled indoors looked rather sorry by winter's end.

Fortunately, by the mid-nineteenth century, the houseplant's plight began to improve as glass became cheaper and more readily available. By 1894, when our house went up, builders were putting in windows galore.

Our house might be sunny, but it's also drafty. We've grown accustomed to spending a good part of the year walking around in our woollies, but tropical houseplants protest. Rather than turning up the thermostat, we crowd all the tropicals into one relatively toasty room and give the rest of the windows over to herbs. They're a pleasant alternative and, with few exceptions, they welcome the cold reception.

Although our household has no qualms about growing plants solely for their beauty, the herbs pull their weight in other ways as well. Most are plucked regularly to season our suppers. Others impart aromatherapy when we walk by, reach over, rub their leaves, and release their pungent perfume into the surrounding atmosphere—it's the only air freshener that we permit within our walls. Even the myrtle (*Myrtus communis* 'Microphylla') has its purpose. The foliage has only a slight scent when crushed and I've yet to find a recipe that calls for myrtle, but my uncle swears that eating one little purple

This sun-drenched windowbox brims with Origanum pulchellum *'Kent Beauty'.*

berry daily eases his arthritis. I'm not sure whether the relief is actual or imagined, but it's a great excuse to nurture a rather comely herb nearby.

Not all herbs make exemplary houseplants. Sweet basil (*Ocimum basilicum*) is a stinker to grow indoors—the stems become woody, the foliage drops, and suddenly you're left with a plant that is useless for any sort of culinary application. Summer savory (*Satureja hortensis*) is equally worthless indoors, although its winter counterpart, *S. montana*, is a splendid stand-in. Tarragon (*Artemisia dracunculus*) slips into dormancy over the winter. (It doesn't look particularly handsome in summertime, either.) Lemon verbena (*Aloysia triphylla*) drops its foliage at the slightest hint of a chill and spends the rest of winter in dormancy. I forgive a few fallen leaves, however, for the sake of its incomparable lemon scent. Lemon grass (*Cymbopogon citratus*), on the other hand, looks so disarmingly akin to an overgrown lawn weed that most folks prefer not to feature it on the windowsill. With these few exceptions, most other herbs are perfectly suited to life on the sill.

Rather than leaving you stranded with a million choices, I'll suggest a few personal favorites. For example, no home would be complete without rosemary. You might fail with rosemary time after time, but you feel compelled to try again. Apparently, rosemary has a long history of frequent failures. In fact, there's an old English adage concerning homegrown rosemary: "If rosemary thriveth, the woman ruleth." Although I have no intention of disrupting the balance of power in your household, it's my duty to offer some thumbnotes on rosemary. First of all, there are several different varieties available, so choose one with a shape that fits your situation. The smallest is *Rosmarinus officinalis* 'Blue Boy', which stands only six to twelve inches tall and spends most of the year topped by blue blossoms. 'Prostrata' and 'Collingwood Ingram' are small-leaved and sprawling, whereas 'Lockwood de Forest', 'Golden Rain', 'Albiflorus', and our own 'Logee Blue' are bolt upright and make excellent topiaries.

A pantry window ledge is an ideal spot for a culinary collection such as this potpourri of (left to right) Pelargonium 'True Rose' (rose-scented geranium), Origanum vulgare 'Variegata' (variegated oregano), Marrubium incanum (horehound), and Rosmarinus officinalis (rosemary).

Rosemary demands cool temperatures at night. When the thermometer shoots above 55 degrees Fahrenheit after dark, it begins to look straggly. It requires a south-facing window and more humidity than most herbs. Our rosemary resides in the sizable south window of a frequently steamed-up bathroom. Good air circulation will keep mildew (which looks like silver powder) from enshrouding the leaves. But the most difficult feat is watering. Rosemary doesn't mind a slight wilt, but when left too dry it will drop its needles. The balance is tricky to achieve.

In addition to rosemary, all sorts of other herbs can be kept handy for culinary purposes. Since culinary herbs are trimmed continually, you can easily crowd a few favorites together in an herbal window box without fear of the bedfellows elbowing one another. For a small box, you might try oregano (*Origanum vulgare* subsp. *hirtum*), marjoram (*Origanum vulgare*), thyme (upright thymes such as *Thymus vulgaris* or any of its hybrids are best), parsley (the curly varieties are most compact), winter savory, and sage (*Salvia officinalis*). But, of course, if other herbs are frequently thrown into your saucepan, give them space in the window box.

Some herbs won't thrive in the cramped quarters of a window box, but they do fine solo. Although starter plants of sweet bay (*Laurus nobilis*) might seem deceptively small, they quickly add stature. In two years you'll have a small tree and can begin harvesting a few aromatic leaves. Meanwhile, your sweet bay might take up space but it doesn't monopolize much time. Bays rarely need repotting or pruning. They require very little water and demand only modest fertilizing. When you consider the price of bay leaves, it's an excellent investment.

Although lavender is not a common cooking herb, it has a long tradition indoors. According to Izaac Walton's *The Compleat Angler*, English lavender (*Lavandula angustifolia*) was once placed in the windows of wayside taverns to signify that the linens were clean. Ever since, the soapy scent that floats from lavender has established a cozy association with home. If you plan to continue the tradition, the trick

Few flower colors equal the brilliant sky blue of Rosmarinus officinalis *(center). Here it is framed by* Leptospermum scoparium *'Ruby Glow' (left) and* Streptosolen jamesonii.

to growing lavender in a pot is pruning. Without a drastic annual haircut, your lavender will exhibit scandalously naked ankles rather than tufts of tight new growth. You'll also increase the heft of those handsome purple flower spikes by pruning in early spring.

In addition to English lavender and its hybrids, there are nonhardy lavenders that are equally worthy of windowsill space. Each has its own distinct aroma, released when you brush the foliage and also when sunbeams fall heavily on the leaves. When French lavender (*Lavandula dentata*), *L. latifolia*, and Spanish lavender (*L. stoechas*) are sitting at your elbow, you'll find yourself sampling and comparing their scents.

By all rights, mints shouldn't be included here. Mints are herbs, of course, but they certainly don't demand a sunny window to survive. In most cases, an east or west sill will suffice, and the same is true for the closely related lemon balm (*Melissa officinalis*) and catnip (*Nepeta cataria*). As long as you apply water generously, root prune frequently, and shear their tops every three months, mints make delightful houseplants. Because children have a special fascination for spearmint and peppermint, mints are a great way to begin nurturing a green thumb.

If mints are for kids, then patchouli (*Pogostemon heyneanus*) is ideal for teenagers. Anyone who has come within two blocks of a Grateful Dead concert has already been introduced to the aroma of patchouli perfume. Fortunately, the foliage features a slightly toned-down version of the bottled stuff. If you possess a sunny windowsill and a watering can, you can have that scent right at your fingertips. Even the rebellious youth in your family can keep patchouli in fine fettle. But one word of caution: Rub patchouli on your body as much as you desire, but don't eat the leaves—patchouli is poisonous.

The world is filled with many herbs, and most are worthy of adoption indoors. Given the diversity, it's impossible to offer a single set of cultural rules to cover all the bases. However, most herbs have a few common denominators. For example, they tend to prefer cool temperatures and abundant sun. In fact, their essential oils gain pungency with intense light. Nutrition also affects an herb's aroma. Herbs prefer a lean, limy soil, and their scent becomes muted when they are overfed. After that, they all go their own separate ways for whims and fancies.

Herbs make an excellent foil for a south windowsill filled with flowers. Of course, blossoms are a bonus on some herbs such as rosemary and thyme, but the foliage is the main draw. And herbs can easily be turned into living sculpture. With a little imagination and a pair of pruners, you can clip them into whimsical forms, making the windowsill an artistic year-round extension of the garden outside.

Hibiscus

When customers wanted a plant that blooms year-round with brightly colored flowers the size of dinner plates, I used to send them away empty-handed. Now, without skipping a beat, I turn around and suggest hibiscus. For gardeners who demand the impossible, they're just the ticket.

It all started with *Hibiscus rosa-sinensis*, popularly known as the rose of China, a densely foliated shrub with abundant two- to five-inch flowers in rosy shades. Early in the game, a very floriferous semidouble hybrid appeared, which the Victorians called *H. rosa-sinensis pleno*. This plant later evolved into the frilly, pompomlike doubles and cup-and-saucer shapes that we know today. But fiddling with the flower forms was just the beginning.

In the plant shop business, hibiscus have monopolized the limelight for a century or more. Recognizing a potential gold mine, breeders have recently beefed up hibiscus, increasing their flower size until each blossom spreads a foot wide when fully unfurled. Half a dozen years ago, the plant world was all agog when a handful of these buxom hibiscus burst onto the scene. Now there are well over one thousand hybrids on the market. Not content merely to swell the blossom size, the hybridizers also expanded their range of color to include every shade of pink, a complete repertoire of reds including dark burgundy, yellows from muted honey to glowing canary yellow, oranges, lavenders, and blues. Often several shades adorn the same blossom in rings or splotches that appear as if someone randomly splattered a paintbrush over their surface. Frankly, these new hibiscus tend to look a little unreal. The other day, I saw a photo of a patriotic red, white, and true-blue striped hibiscus. I still wonder whether the Hibiscus Society was pulling my leg.

Although hibiscus blossom year-round, each flower doesn't last long. In the past, all hibiscus opened their paper-thin blossoms for only a day. Although breeders haven't increased the duration drastically, there are a few new hybrids that linger a bit longer. The rainbow-colored blossoms of 'Donna Lynn', and the golden-petaled 'Toronto', for example, remain open nearly two days.

Without a doubt, hibiscus come in some fairly outlandish colors, but there's a clean-cut tidiness about hibiscus that prevents them from appearing vulgar. In this case, big *is* beautiful. And although hibiscus are sold at every corner florist shop, they haven't become a cliché. Many seasoned gardeners vie for the latest hybrids, and some even dabble in breeding. It's simple enough to do. If hand-pollinated, hibiscus set seed readily. When the seed is dry, nick its rounded top, plant it, and wait one to three weeks for germination.

It's hard to go wrong with hibiscus. Even if you rarely fertilize, seldom repot, and never prune your plant, it will still look presentable. But it won't be ravishing and it will wilt with vexatious regularity. If you want something ravishing, you'll have to apply the pruning shears. When allowed to grow unchecked, hibiscus send out a single stem stretching eight feet into the air, with a constant supply of blossoms at the very top. By forfeiting flowers for a few months and pruning to encourage branching, you'll eventually have bountiful blossoms on a three-foot plant.

For a while, everyone wanted "dwarf" hibiscus. In truth, there's no such thing. Those squat plants sold at flower shops aren't genetically dwarfed; they're actually ordinary hibiscus treated with a growth retardant to keep them diminutive. The most popular growth controls for hibiscus are Bonzi ™ and Cycocel. When cuttings are two months old and have already been pinched to induce branching, they're sprayed with two to four applications of a growth control spaced three to four weeks apart. Immediately after treatment the plant gets greener, it produces a multitude of buds, and the growth becomes nice and plump. But the spell doesn't last forever. Without continual applications, a hibiscus will resume its normal stature after six months. And growth retardants aren't without dangers, to you or your plants. It's possible to throw the plant into reverse. A better idea might be to prune vigorously to achieve density.

All hibiscus are dramatic, but the crepe-paper textured petals of Hibiscus rosa-sinensis *'Double Pink' are especially riveting.*

Hibiscus should blossom both summer and winter on a bright, south-facing windowsill. If buds blast before unfurling, it is probably because of insufficient light and warmth. Optimal winter night temperatures are 50 to 65 degrees Fahrenheit, but hibiscus survive with scarcely a whimper when temperatures plummet into the forties. If buds don't form despite sun and warmth, overfeeding might be the problem. Fertilize hibiscus once a month in spring and summer, but drastically decrease both the dosage and frequency during the winter months to once every six to eight weeks.

Like all members of the mallow family, hibiscus are prone to insect infestations. They seem to draw aphids, red spider mites, and white-flies like a magnet. Arm yourself against those foes, since they're bound to visit.

Although we're all atwitter about the giant-flowering hybrids of *H. rosa-sinensis*, there are other family members worthy of note. Fancy foliage isn't a feature of most hibiscus, but *H. rosa-sinensis* 'Cooperi', known as the checkerboard plant, has long, thin, white-marbled foliage streaked with blush red. It blooms prolifically and the cherry flowers enhance the foliar colors.

From the foliage, it's easy to guess the familial affiliation of *H. schizopetalus* at first glance. The flowers, however, hardly resemble other members of the clan. Commonly known as Japanese lanterns, the striking orange-and-pink blossoms dangle down but curve their feathered petals upward like wings in flight. Those unique blossoms come by the dozen during the summer months.

Perhaps someday we'll have a catchy nickname for *Anisodontea hypomandarum* and its fame will eclipse its cousin, the hibiscus. Even saddled with its cumbersome binomial, anisodontea has attracted a crowd of admirers. Throughout the year it produces countless inch-wide pink blossoms against small, compact leaves. Compared to hibiscus, the flowers might be modest, but they have a winning cheeriness and dependability. Set beside a few full-scale hibiscus, those tiny but plentiful blossoms provide a perfect accent to tone down the knock-'em-dead impact of their inflated cousins.

Mandevillas

Nowadays, mandevillas can be found adorning every picket fence on Long Island, and they are featured in every gardening gift catalog under the sun on the strength of their summer splendor. But we've always had one growing in our window year-round. There it is, wound neatly on its trellis, looking every bit as exuberant as anything you'd encounter outside.

The mandevilla that took up residence on our windowsill was *Mandevilla ×amabilis* 'Alice du Pont', a sizable vine with comely oval, pleated leaves crowned by clusters of immense rosy trumpets. In my book, it's still the handsomest member of the family. Half the beauty of the plant stems from the poetry of its progression: Each five-petaled trumpet unfurls from a tightly wound bud into a porcelain-pink, frilly-edged blossom with overlapping petals. Shy at first, the blossom expands and its color blushes deeper with time, accented and enhanced by the paler shades of newly opened buds in the cluster. As if that weren't enough, there's always the filigree of fresh growth and some young leaves to punctuate the statement.

Actually, *M. ×amabilis* 'Alice du Pont' first came into our house under a different name. We knew the vine as *Dipladenia amoena* 'Alice du Pont', and some nurseries still offer it under that name although the classification was changed in the 1970s. I'm generally no fan of nomenclature changes, but the new designation, which honors Henry John Mandeville, a nineteenth-century British minister to Buenos Aires, rolls nicely off the tongue and somehow seems more appropriate for this majestic vine. The hybrid 'Alice du Pont' originated at Longwood Gardens in Pennsylvania, apparently an offspring of *M. splendens*, although its exact parentage is uncertain.

For a good portion of the year *M.* 'Alice du Pont' is as close to flawless as nature gets. The vine is invariably tidy, bug-free (except for mealybugs, which attack anything), and absolutely ravishing. Its sole fault is that the dense foliage blocks the light, leading to a one-sided blossom display in a windowsill. That's why our plant dwells in the bay window where light enters from several angles. In winter *M.* 'Alice du Pont' often goes into a brief lull during which it garners strength for future performances. It's a brief hiatus, so don't panic if a few leaves are shed—the vine will sprout new ones soon enough.

We seize the moment to trim back dead wood, rewind the vine, or repot. Before we know it, the buds are swelling again.

Mandevilla 'Alice du Pont' is the superstar in the family, but *M. sanderi* 'Red Riding Hood' comes a close second. The species itself, a native of Brazil, boasts small, shiny copper leaves, whiplike growth, and a smattering of two- to three-inch-wide, pink trumpet-shaped blossoms accented by yellow throats. The vine is compact, tidy, and bug-free. Nevertheless, *M. sanderi* definitely plays a supporting role to the eye-popping, lipstick-red, yellow-throated blossoms of *M.* 'Red Riding Hood'. Always in blossom, *M.* 'Red Riding Hood' is more compact than its parent, and has a much looser growth habit than its scaled-up cousin, *M.* 'Alice du Pont'. Depending upon its early training, the growth can either assume an upright stature or trail down, but it is always capped by those riotous blossoms.

Personally, I find *M.* 'Red Riding Hood' to be a little overbearing colorwise. For day-to-day living, I prefer *M. boliviensis* at my elbow. This species shows more of the family's characteristic fastidiousness, with long, slender, shiny leaves on loose, vining branches. As its name reveals, *M. boliviensis* is native to Bolivia and Ecuador, and bears luminous, tubular, sparkling white blossoms, each accented by a deep butter-yellow throat. The blossoms are only two inches wide but they open in abundance through most of the year. In winter, the flowers thin out to a few lingering clusters during the darkest days. Like its kin, *M. boliviensis* is trouble-free.

Mandevilla laxa (formerly known as *M. suaveolens*) also has white blossoms, but they lack the yellow central marking. Instead, each pearly blossom has frilly petals with delicate creases in the throat. Best of all, *M. laxa*'s blossoms emit a heady lilylike scent, which has earned it the nickname Chilean jasmine. As far as I know, *M. laxa* is the only fragrant mandevilla. (Some writers have mistakenly claimed that *M.* 'Alice du Pont' possesses an aroma, but in fact it is absolutely scentless no matter what time of day or night the blossoms are sampled.)

For windowsill purposes, *M. laxa* has one major drawback—it goes totally dormant during the winter. No matter how warm you keep

—

Throughout the year, Mandevilla sanderi *'Red Riding Hood' produces lipstick-red blossoms.*

your home, the vine will die back in autumn leaving nary a stick, and new growth won't reappear until late spring. By midsummer, the fragile twining stems and long slender leaves will again be crowned by numerous flower clusters.

A near relative, *Urichites lutea*, has recently appeared on the indoor/outdoor scene. An extraordinarily robust vine, it makes haste to send thick, shiny-leaved branches racing up any support within grasp. In spring, summer, and fall, quantities of primrose-yellow trumpets bedeck the pale-green foliage. In autumn, when windowsill flowers are few, its abundance is particularly welcome.

Most mandevillas become quite sizable and will monopolize a good chunk of your windowsill in short order. *Mandevilla* 'Red Riding Hood' is the one exception, growing slowly to reach a maximum two to three feet. Other mandevillas will produce three to four feet of energetic growth. They may fill a window, but the space is well invested.

Since mandevillas all prefer warm temperatures, we try not to let the thermometer slip much below 63 degrees Fahrenheit during the winter. Besides that one request, their preferences are few. They aren't thirsty vines. In fact, I can't recall ever seeing a mandevilla wilt, although I'm sure that the leaves would flag under dire circumstances. On the other hand, they dislike a soggy potting medium. Be sure to let the vine dry out between waterings, especially during the winter. We feed our mandevillas moderately, applying fertilizer only once every four to six weeks from March until November. We have also found that mandevillas respond appreciatively to frequent upgradings in pot size, and so we repot when the leaves turn pale in hunger.

Nowadays mandevillas are sold as summer annuals in many garden centers. Thanks to their rampant growth, it's a job that they perform well. Because of this wonderful association with summer, their windowsill performance in midwinter is especially magical. If you block out the dull scene outdoors and concentrate only on the vine framing the view, mandevillas make summer bloom eternal.

Oxalis

I blow hot and cold on oxalis. There are moments when I think they're one of the windowsill's most desirable inhabitants. But then there are times when I consider them to be indoor gardening's greatest eyesores. I guess that my viewpoint has a lot to do with their stage of development and the species in question. Needless to say, I'm not speaking of those noxious weeds that take over the planet. The oxalis I have in mind are native to South America or South Africa. Some are fruitful and multiply shamelessly, but they can't survive a frost—these are strictly indoor plants.

Basically, tender oxalis fit into two groups. The bulbous types are by far the most popular. When bulbous oxalis first sprout, they look like a crop of clover, giving the windowsill a backyardsy feeling. Not long afterward, they blossom with yellow, pink, wine, or white five-petaled flowers. At that point, they're showstoppers in anyone's book. With bright sun, you can sustain that level of excellence for a few months. Then it's downhill.

Among the bulbous types, there are summer-growing varieties, winter-growing types, and a few rhizomatous oxalis that grow continually throughout the year. When the seasonal oxalis aren't performing, they're dormant. Needless to say, for windowsill purposes, it's the winter-growing and blooming types that have the most admirers.

Not many oxalis have acquired nicknames, but *O. purpurea* was awarded the catchy sobriquet grand duchess so that it could be successfully marketed as a Christmas or Valentine's Day gift plant. For that purpose, lavender and white forms were perfected to add to the standard pink. In autumn, florists nestle five or six bulbs of different colored grand duchess bulbs together in four-inch pots to achieve a harlequin effect. Actually, the goal is to sell the pots before the flowers open. The leaves are lightly felted, very delicate in texture, and set in threesomes; the blossoms are one and a half inches wide and so fragile that a brisk breeze will crease their petals.

Oxalis brasiliensis also has shamrocklike leaves and—wouldn't you know it—the wine-red blossoms open just in time for St. Patrick's Day. The leaves of this species look incredibly cloveresque, they stand only three to four inches from the ground when grown in good light,

and they're much sturdier in texture than the grand duchess. The display lasts several months in picture-perfect condition.

From its foliage, *O. hirta* scarcely seems like one of the family. In winter, the bulbs sprout in tufts with many long, thin leaves circling around. Without superabundant light and rather parched soil underfoot, those tufts begin to stretch and wind up looking quite unkempt. But in an ultra-sunny windowsill, they form mossy little clumps topped by rosy blossoms, each accented by a creamy eye.

As soon as the winter oxalis shrivel up and bow out, summer oxalis bulbs begin to grow. If you plant bulbs of *O. bowiei* in spring, they immediately send up trios of large, shiny leaves; not long thereafter clusters of inch-wide shocking-pink blossoms follow. Standing one to two feet high if you include the flower scapes, *O. bowiei* is taller than most bulbous types. But it uses the space wisely, competing favorably with other summer attractions.

Unfortunately, the summer-growing *O. pes-caprae* isn't equally adept at holding its own against the seasonal fare. Known as the Bermuda buttercup, this is the same infamous oxalis that took Bermuda by storm and now runs rampant over southern Florida and warm regions of California. The bulbs increase with embarrassing fecundity, sprouting long-stemmed leaves crowned by bunches of button-size, sunray-yellow blossoms. The flowers reputedly have a scent, but the aroma is not particularly noteworthy. At one time, a double version known as 'Flore Pleno' was available, with many-petaled blossoms that emit an enhanced fragrance. Now the double version is nearly impossible to find.

Recently, *O. tetraphylla* (formerly *O. deppei*), known as the lucky clover, has eclipsed all other summer types. Actually, *O. tetraphylla* has only traveled on the coattails of its bronze-leaved hybrid called 'Iron Cross'. Although each of the leaf stems of 'Iron Cross' stand six inches or more in height, the excess length is compensated for by eye-catching burgundy markings. The leaves come in fours, hence the lucky clover connection, and the markings make each leaf look like a Maltese cross. The wine-colored blossoms aren't really the main attraction, but they certainly add to the show. To counteract the long-

Unlike most of its kin, Oxalis magellanica *'Nelson' creeps along the ground forming a mass of tiny cloverlike leaves. Occasionally, frilly, double white flowers appear.*

legged leaf stems, tuck the bulbs closely together so each sprout supports its neighbors.

A number of rhizomatous oxalis are classified with the bulbous types, but have given up the bad habit of going dormant. By far the best known is *O. regnellii* from South America, with sharply cut, triangular leaves in sets of three. Standing neatly four to six inches high and frequently accented by white blossoms, it's a pretty sight. And it stays that way—there's no hideous predormancy scenario to anticipate. As if *O. regnellii* weren't good enough, now there's also an unnamed hybrid with silver-centered triangular leaves. But it pales in comparison to the newest rage. *Oxalis regnellii* recently fostered a flaming-pink-leaved version called 'Atropurpurea', prominently displayed in every garden center.

From the moment you plant bulbous oxalis (and they must be popped into the soil when the first signs of growth appear in spring or autumn), they should be drenched in sun. Without abundant light, the first sprouts will stretch, ruining the entire season's display. Don't even consider oxalis unless you've got a bright south window.

Beyond sun, bulbous oxalis prefer a heavy, sandy soil. Most varieties should be planted an inch deep. Give them a generous soak when they're planted, then let the soil go rather dry until growth emerges. Water lightly, always allowing them to dry out between drinks, and fertilize once every three weeks while they're in the full flush of growth.

Like most bulbous plants, there's nothing you can do to tidy up an oxalis once it starts to decline. When dormancy calls, those pitiful yellowing leaves and floppy stems must be tolerated until they finally brown, dry up, and drop off. Only then can the bulbs be stashed out of sight, out of mind. You can try to hasten the process by withholding water. As the leaves dry, let the soil parch. When all growth has withered, take up the bulbs, put them in a paper bag, and store them in a cool, dark place.

Less often grown but easier to handle are the tree-type oxalis. Don't be thrown off by the arboreal imagery. Tree oxalis are so called be-

In a sunny Gothic window sit a pair of Oxalis ortgiesii *standards with* Oxalis regnellii *'Atropurpurea' (left foreground) and* Oxalis crassipes *'Alba' (right foreground).*

cause they grow continuously and make upright stems. They don't turn into trees, or anything close to it. They all have small yellow blossoms that often appear in profusion, primarily in summer. But it's their foliage, not their flowers, that won them a spot on the windowsill.

A good example is *O. vulcanicola* (formerly *O. siliquosa*), which has plump reddish stems and quantities of tiny green and blush-red leaves. It makes a riveting hanging basket plant, especially in midsummer when the yellow blossoms are plentiful. *Oxalis ortgiesii* is even more elaborate, with deeply textured purple and copper leaves, each accented by a fishtail-shaped edge. In good light, the yellow blossoms appear year-round. *Oxalis herrerae* has plain green leaves but its growth habit holds your eye. In fact, when *O. herrerae* is grown very dry, it masquerades as a succulent. The leaf stems swell, looking rather bloated compared to the minute leaflets on each tip. Finally, there's the fire fern. *Oxalis hedysaroides* 'Rubra' has fragile, deep-maroon branches and leaf stems that hold equally delicate teardrop-shaped maroon leaves at arm's length. No one imagines that the ultra-exotic fire fern is actually an oxalis until they catch sight of the signature five-petaled yellow blossoms.

Like all tree-type oxalis, the fire fern looks smashing if it's strictly pruned. Start disciplining tree-type oxalis very young before the stems become woody. And keep cutting them back—that's the only way to induce branching and maintain quality. The soil should be sandy and heavy, the roots should be cramped, and drinks should be served only when the soil is quite dry. (Oxalis rarely wilt.) Oxalis respond gratefully when they're treated (or mistreated) like cacti.

Oxalis can be ravishing or revolting. Depending upon when you catch them, how much light you provide, and how careful you are with water, they can spend their growing season looking like cabbages or kings. Of all the plants on your south window, oxalis appreciate sun the most. They are an excellent investment in solar energy.

Passionflowers

Nothing moves like passionflowers—they climb with an avidity that leaves other vines groveling in the dust. Let a passionflower loose indoors, turn your back for a moment, and the curtain rod will be engulfed by clutching tendrils, the living room will be lost in meandering greenery. A breathless urgency surrounds this vine. Keeping abreast of a passionflower's acrobatics can be an exhausting occupation by any gardener's standards, but most of us agree that it's worth the effort.

The vine's headstrong ways may be engrossing—even alarming—but the blossoms are absolutely dumbfounding. Picture broad waxen petals, often spanning three to four inches in diameter, in eye-riveting shades of pink, blue, royal purple, or vibrant red. Overlay those petals with a thick crown of contrasting filaments accented by protruding pistils and stamens. Then add an intoxicating aroma—an elixir reminiscent of lilies steeped in sweet peas. Passionflowers bear the sort of blossoms that Hollywood might dream up. And, if the whole shebang seems a little absurd even in this age of overwrought imagination, then consider what Rome must have thought when a monk brought back the first sketch of a passionflower from South America in the early 1600s. Everyone assumed it was a hoax.

Of course, the flower did exist. And when that fact was finally verified, Rome was abuzz with the possibilities inherent in this divine New World plant. Where less devout souls might see only a bizarre bloom, religious scholars recognized all sorts of symbolic meaning. Passionflowers were immediately recruited as visual aids for South American missionaries struggling to demonstrate the passion story to potential converts. According to their interpretation, the ten petals and sepals represented the ten apostles present at the crucifixion, minus Peter and Judas. The filaments imitated the crown of thorns or halo, the five anthers depicted Jesus' five wounds, and the three stigmas stood for the three nails used in the crucifixion.

Nowadays, in a world gone commercial, purveyors of tropical punch and exotic perfumes prefer to play up more amorous connotations of the word *passion*. Ironically, the foliage is actually used to brew sleep-promoting teas that might effectively squelch any passion-

ate overtures. No matter. Most gardeners don't spend much time pondering the vine's religious or romantic associations.

There are many good reasons to patronize passionflowers, some of them gastronomical. Certain species produce tart, custardy passion fruit, which is an important commercial crop in Florida and California. But harvesting fruit isn't really feasible on a windowsill. The two fruit-producing species, *Passiflora quadrangularis* and *P. edulis*, don't make good houseplants. *Passiflora quadrangularis*, known as the giant granadilla, is much too large for the average home. *Passiflora edulis*, the purple granadilla, is not quite so rampant but rarely blooms or sets fruit on a windowsill. Forget the passion fruit and strive for bountiful flowers instead.

The most fulfilling passionflower for the average windowsill is *P. vitifolia*, with immense fire-engine-red blossoms. All passion blooms remain open merely a day, but the most floriferous varieties, such as *P. vitifolia*, produce a continual succession of flowers. As the name suggests, *P. vitifolia*'s leaves look for all the world like grape foliage, and the vine wanders hither and yon with similar abandon. Native to Venezuela, *P. vitifolia* has thick leathery leaves rarely visited by the whiteflies and red spider mites that tend to pester its kin.

For windowsill purposes, it's best to steer away from the other readily available red passionflower, *P. coccinea*, which bears cherry-red blossoms almost identical to *P. vitifolia* in color and form. In our experience, *P. coccinea* is disappointing when contained in a pot or confined to a windowsill. Its blossoms are produced bountifully only when it is grown in a greenhouse and given unrestricted root room underfoot.

Although the red passionflowers are relative newcomers to the indoor scene, others have a long-standing tradition inside. If someone mentions passionflowers without specifying a species, chances are they're speaking of *P. caerulea*, which has been groping around window frames for well over a century. The lacy, finger-shaped leaves of *P. caerulea* are studded with a continual supply of three- to four-inch white-petaled blossoms overlaid with a thick, deep blue crown. 'Constance Elliott', a glistening pure white version, is just beginning

Not all passionflowers bloom enthusiastically in a windowsill, but Passiflora vitifolia *always seems to have a few promising buds.*

to infiltrate the American market. You can let the vine roam unchecked or train its wayward arms and legs into a wreathlike shape by guiding them around a two-foot wire frame. The vine will grow anywhere, but only a sunny south window encourages a bountiful crop of blossoms. And those blossoms will continue into the dead of winter—if the weather is bright.

Passiflora caerulea has spawned several equally floriferous and windowsill-worthy hybrids. The most popular of these is *P. ×alatocaerulea*, with glove-shaped leaves, a rampageous growth habit, and immense, intensely scented blossoms. The flowers resemble waterlily blossoms, with thick alternating pink-and-white petals overlaid by a purple-striped crown that looks like bristling sea urchin spines.

Fairly new on this side of the Atlantic, *P.* 'Jeannette' is another *P. caerulea* cross with more densely packed blossoms than its parent. The fragrant flowers have pink petals overlaid by a broad, wavy crown and the vine blossoms bravely even when light levels are low. In fact, I've never seen the plant without a few promising buds waiting to pop open.

There are plenty of other passionflowers in cultivation. In fact, the genus has no fewer than five hundred members, with new species being discovered almost daily. Their diversity is astounding. *Passiflora jorullensis*, a Mexican species, has small but handsome orange-filamented flowers that emit a vigorous smell uncomfortably akin to well-aged gym socks. On the other hand, Mexico is also the home of *P. helleri*, with equally diminutive blossoms that exude the heavenly scent of clover honey. And flowers are not the only item in the passionflower's bag of tricks: Several species are grown primarily for their ornamental foliage. *Passiflora trifasciata* has three-lobed leaves handsomely mottled with pale green. *Passiflora coriacea* bears intriguing nickel-size blossoms in clusters, but the main draw is its majestic batwing-shaped leaves. And *P. coriacea* has another, more practical claim to fame—in Guatemala, its seed is crushed and used as an insecticide against cockroaches. Red spider mites, whiteflies, and even mealybugs avoid this species, although they have an affinity for most members of the family.

⌒

Reliably hardy to USDA Zone 5, Passiflora *'Incense' can be grown indoors or out.*

Like most athletes, passionflowers have a vigorous appetite. Feed them once every two or three weeks in summer with 20-20-20 or any balanced fertilizer. In winter, feed once a month. Although many houseplants prefer to be pot-bound, passionflowers enjoy generous root accommodations, but don't overdo it. When you repot, go up two pot sizes rather than one, and anchor the stem firmly in heavy, rich soil.

Give passionflowers abundant light—sun is the crucial ingredient in flower production. If your plant pauses in its blossom display, you can usually blame it on gloomy weather. Passionflowers are thirsty vines and will wilt quickly when drinks must be served.

I've already mentioned that passionflowers are prone to whiteflies and red spider mites. However, in your search for pests, don't panic at the plant's own method of warding off natural predators. Passionflowers have developed a cunning trick to confuse their primary foe. Tiny yellow dots freckle the leaf surfaces to fool heliconius butterflies into believing that eggs have already been laid. If that isn't effective, tiny glands on the leaves or stems secrete nectar to attract ants, wasps, and flies that prey on heliconius larvae.

There is something endearing about these resourceful, rambunctious vines. True, passionflowers aren't neat little pot plants that sit obediently waiting for a glimpse in their general direction. Forget a passionflower for a few weeks and the vine will come and get you. But when it comes to gardening—indoors or out—I prefer dynamic to dull any day.

Pentas

If you have never heard of pentas, you're not alone, judging from the blank stares that greet any mention of the name. In terms of popularity, this colorful year-round bloomer has a long way to go before it becomes a household word, and yet sometime soon its day may come.

Even when Pentas lanceolata *hybrids are massed together in a large planter, their colors will harmonize beautifully.*

Pentas has potential. Although the folige looks and acts something like heliotrope greenery, with a similar tendency to become leggy, the leaves aren't this plant's main draw. If *Pentas lanceolata* has a shot at fame, it will have to capitalize on its abundant umbels of blossoms. Actually, a century ago, that trait won the plant some modest renown.

In Victorian times, before gardeners settled into a boring diet consisting solely of a few select houseplants, *P. lanceolata* had a brief brush with acclaim. Introduced from East Africa in 1842 and grown as *P. carnea* in the nineteenth century, the species is crowned by umbels of dull buff-colored blossoms. Even so, the flames of interest burned with sufficient fervor to prod breeders to brandish their pollinating brushes. By the beginning of the twentieth century, the color spectrum had expanded to include white (a form known as 'Alba') and lavender (called 'Orchid Star'), as well as several rosy shades blushing from pink to crimson. Before long, florists were also making use of the blossoms as cut flowers. (Cuts last at least a week in a vase.)

After that brief moment in the sun, pentas just slipped into obscurity. Heaven knows why, because pentas is a loyal performer indoors. Despite low humidity and toasty parlor-type temperatures, it grows and blossoms nonstop in a sunny window. And the flowers are every bit as showy as geraniums, with a much longer blooming period. Each three- to five-inch flower head is composed of a constellation of small stars opening slowly over several weeks. And the colors have come a long way from the original nondescript species. They're now absolutely eye-riveting.

If you plan to revive the passion for pentas, be prepared to prune. Gardeners who are afraid to wield pruning shears should never attempt a pentas. Left unchecked, a pentas will form one pathetic umbel atop a single straggly branch. Begin pinching early when the plant is less than six inches tall to encourage widening girth. But don't stop there: Continue pruning and pinching throughout the plant's career. Fertilizing moderately (once a month from March to November) will also prevent stretching. Most of the rose-colored hybrids can be shaped into broad two-foot plants crowned by a bountiful crop of blossoms. 'Alba' and 'Orchid Star' will attain three feet in height, topped by proportionally fatter umbels.

Pentas's tendency to stretch has also recently been overcome with the introduction of several new compact cultivars. 'Tu-Tone' was the first dwarf hybrid to appear, and it undercut everything introduced previously. With just a little encouragement, 'Tu-Tone' begins to expand nicely outward rather than upward. It rarely exceeds a foot in height and is continually spangled with pink blossoms, each streaked by a central white band. 'Tu-Tone' is the only pentas that can be successfully coaxed into hanging basket form.

Even more encouraging for anyone marking the progress of pentas is the recent appearance of the cultivars 'California Lavender' and 'California Pink'. Both bloom in soft pastels so artfully matched that they beg to be grown side by side. They are self-branching if you start them off with a strong initial pinch. The smaller of the pair is 'California Lavender', which remains under a foot in height and is crowned by umbels so plump they nearly hide the foliage. 'California Pink' is only slightly taller with an equally dense crop of flowers.

Unfortunately, pentas shares another unpleasant trait with heliotrope besides a tendency to stretch. Like heliotrope, it also attracts whiteflies from miles around. Red spider mites and mealybugs are not as troublesome, but they're definitely potential problems. Obviously, insects make a beeline for this type of juicy, tender, tempting foliage.

Juicy, tender foliage also wilts easily. Pentas are thirsty plants. You will probably have to water them daily on bright summer days, but periodic repotting should prevent the necessity of serving drinks twice a day during heat waves. It also helps to use a heavy, rich potting soil. In summer, pentas can endure quite hot temperatures with no ill effect as long as their thirst is quenched, a trait that will endear them to gardeners with city terraces or smoldering cement patios. They also tolerate whipping winds and light salt spray. However, during the winter when light levels are low, pentas quickly become gangly when the thermostat is set above 65 degrees Fahrenheit. On the other hand, if the night temperature dips much lower than 55 degrees, the new dwarf hybrids can fall victim to disease.

Granted, pentas aren't perfect. They have problems and challenges, just like most other tropicals. But that's what gardening is all about—outdoors or inside. I would perish of boredom by midwinter if I couldn't play with my pruning shears. Thank goodness, pentas offer plenty of opportunity.

Succulents

Not everyone can muster the 30 percent humidity necessary to nurture houseplants. For those who don't want to fill humidifiers or juggle pebble trays, there's a group of plants that can tolerate parchingly dry growing conditions—the succulents. These plants thrive when moisture is scarce both in the atmosphere and underfoot. Forget to water them for a week or more and they'll thank you for it; leave town on business for a few days and there's no need to hire a plantsitter. Succulents are thus the perfect choice for absentee indoor gardeners.

As far as I can tell, the definition of a succulent is nearly as nebulous as the concept of what constitutes an herb. Aeoniums, crassulas, echeverias, sedums, sempervivum, and other members of the family Crassulaceae compose the bulk of the group referred to as succulents. In addition, some of the more grotesque members of the euphorbia family are considered succulents, and several gnarled pelargonium species are also lumped into the same group. Although these plants aren't all related, they share an ability to store moisture in their leaves and stems to tide them over during dry periods. In addition to providing a practical survival tactic, those reservoirs often assume fascinating shapes and forms. Typically, succulents have swollen leaves and stems with a thick protective surface. Sometimes those leaf surfaces are soft, as in the cub's paw (*Cotyledon ladysmithiensis*), which has thick rounded foliage covered with plush, pea-green felt, and the panda plant (*Kalanchoe tomentosa*), which sports long, thin, puffy leaves clad with white fur. On the other hand, many euphorbias bristle with thorns. In addition to their varied textures, succulent leaves appear in a broad spectrum of colors, especially blues, silver, white, and rose.

But fancy leaves are not the only virtue of these plants. Many succulents are eager bloomers, and they don't confine their performance to the sunny summer months. If blossoms are your goal, the kalanchoes are the best of the bunch. Their floral display comes during the short-

Blossoms always add distinction to the decor. In this sunny window sit the Easter cactus Schlumbergera truncata 'Gold Charm' (right) and the Australian herb Correa reflexa 'Pink' (left).

est days of the year, when you desperately need a botanical boost. The most common kalanchoe is the flaming Katy (*K. blossfeldiana*), widely sold for Christmas in several glistening pastel shades. Nothing could be easier to grow. In fact, flaming Katy doesn't even need a south window—an east- or west-facing window will do.

Not quite so omnipresent but just as eye-riveting is *K. pumila*, with its midwinter display of plump blue-green rosettes, each tipped by sparkling pink flowers. An equally dazzling wintertime performer is *K. uniflora*, with dangling chains of heart-shaped leaves smothered by hundreds of inch-long, balloonlike, salmon-colored blossoms. Both species require a sun-drenched south window to keep their foliage in tight rosettes. All kalanchoes blossom most reliably if grown in a room where the lights are left off during the evening.

The crassulas combine dainty leaves in small, ground-hugging rosettes with a cloud of frilly flowers. My favorites are *Crassula cooperi*, with half-inch-long, thin, speckled leaves in clusters that get covered in autumn with a fluff of pale pink flowers held just above the foliage, and *C. schmidtii*, with deep-green leaves that stick straight up in small pointed colonies and are crowned by rose-colored flowers. The creeping crassulas are cute, but the best-known member of the genus is the upscale *C. ovata* (formerly *C. argentea*), known far and wide as the jade plant. Among an easy batch of relatives, the jade plant is particularly simple to grow. Aside from some pruning to keep the oval-leaved, thick stems branching right and left, jade plants are virtually carefree. However, the creeping crassulas require some precautions. The trick lies in keeping the foliage absolutely dry when you water the soil, and letting the soil become nearly parched before watering again.

Sedums are so similar in appearance to crassulas that it's difficult for most of us to tell the difference. In many cases, sedums also form little rosettes of brittle, bloated leaves that either creep along the ground or form tufts on thick branches. They aren't as eager to bloom as crassulas, but the foliage is quite intriguing. The best known member of the genus is the donkey's tail (*Sedum morganianum*), with ropelike chains of fat little silver leaves that shed whenever the plant is slightly jostled. Fortunately, each of those dislodged orbs can be

In the depths of winter, the colorful flowers of Kalanchoe blossfeldiana, *or flaming Katy, spring up in the driest environment.*

planted in sand with the end that was once attached to the stem facing downward. Eventually, after several months' wait, a new rosette will pop up and a new donkey's tail is born.

Many folks who are not particularly fond of succulents nevertheless fall for echeverias. They are an astonishingly diverse group of plants. Most echeverias form rosettes that look like pinecones, but each plays its own variation on that theme. Some of the more noteworthy variations include *Echeveria gibbiflora* 'Carnuculata', known as the chicken-gizzard plant for the weirdly shaped growths that erupt from its blue-green foliage. *Echeveria crenulata* is blue-green with pink scalloped edging on each leaf; *E.* 'Hoveyi' has silver streaks running the length of its thin leaves. Best of all, most echeverias send up tall, candelabralike stems of waxy flowers in vivid hues. Echeverias are so easy to grow that the main challenge is keeping abreast of their progress. Older plants tend to put so much weight on one side of their pot that the container topples continually. Although you can prune an echeveria to alleviate this problem, it's better to cut it all the way back to the base and let it sprout anew.

Succulents may be among the easiest plants to adapt indoors, but they do have their druthers. All of these plants are sun-lovers. Native to the deserts of the world, they do more than merely pout when light levels are low. In a dimly lit window, most succulents will quickly turn to mush. Similarly, they all abhor overwatering, and will react to this insult with stem rot. The affliction usually begins at the base, so there's no reviving a plant once it's been struck. If you're a heavy-handed waterer, succulents are not for you.

The trick is to water only when the soil is quite dry to the touch in summer, and to water even less frequently in winter. Weeks can slip by before a succulent gardener is called upon to dispense a single drop. When you do water, hand out the drinks early in the morning on a sunny day. Even then, watering is tricky business in winter— serious succulent growers use fans to keep moisture from settling on stems and leaves.

Naturally, soil plays a crucial role in the watering issue. Succulents all like to sink their roots into a sandy, well-drained soil. To be on the safe side, mix your potting medium with an equal measure of sand. A layer of pebbles on the bottom of the pot will also help wick away water, while a pebble top-dressing will keep moisture from collecting around the stem. Choose unglazed clay pots rather than plastic containers, and always keep the roots slightly cramped. In most cases, a shallow container is preferable.

Most succulents need only modest feeding and then only in summer. Use generously diluted 20-20-20 formula and apply it once every four to six weeks. Some zygocactus, otherwise known as Thanksgiving and Christmas cacti, occasionally exhibit a disquieting yellowing and streaking problem. Experts aren't quite sure of the cause, but they caution against using excessive fertilizer to green up the foliage again. A superabundance of iron may be the culprit. If so, leaching the soil with plain water will provide a cure.

In their native habitats, succulents withstand a broad range of temperatures and fluctuations in weather. In summer, they luxuriate when the mercury soars; in winter they prefer chilly temperatures around 50 degrees Fahrenheit but will survive much warmer environments. If you have a sunny porch protected from sudden downpours, send your succulents outdoors in summer—you might see blossoms on plants that never bloomed before.

Ground-covering succulents should be divided every few years. Taller plants such as euphorbias and kalanchoes must be pruned to encourage branching. The best practice is to prune before they scrape the ceiling—older wood takes forever to send out side shoots. After pruning, some growers suggest dusting the wound with a fungicide to prevent tip rot. To be on the safe side, never prune or repot during damp, cloudy weather.

Introduction

One of the sweetest times of day comes when the morning sun first sends its rays through our east-facing windows. It's early, the rays seem very golden indeed, and their welcome warmth dispels the morning chill. Part of the beauty is the suddenness of it all. One moment the light is diffuse and nebulous, the next moment everything is on fire. In winter, when I tend to be a tad lazy, I nonetheless hurry to get up on sunny mornings, open the shades, and give the early rays unobstructed entry so they can work their magic on the plants waiting inside.

The first sunbeams of the morning glisten on the leaves of houseplants like an ocean of crystals. For an hour or two the light is fairly intense. In fact, in the heat of the summer, we draw the shades to preserve the coolness in the room for a few precious hours. But drawn curtains aren't necessary to shield the bloomers within—those morning sunbeams do the plants no harm. Even in high summer, the intensity is short-lived in an east-facing sill. Just as quickly as it came, the light subsides into diffuse brightness again. Then it's time to water the plants and move on to the other chores of the day.

Most plants that grow in east windows could just as easily thrive on a west-facing sill. I find, though, that east is a bit brighter, especially in winter. Even on the shortest days of the year, there's good light streaming through east-facing panes until noon or shortly thereafter. And if your eastern sill gets a glint of southerly rays, it can garner quite a generous supply of sunbeams. So I fill our east windows with plants that don't demand full sun but require good light nonetheless.

Compared to the riot of color in southern exposures, east windows are fairly subdued. Clivias, angel-wing begonias, and orchids are typical of the staid and sophisticated botanicals that make their home here. And perhaps coincidentally, east windows tend to be filled with hefty houseplants. Rather than a battalion of little wonders, our east-facing windows host a few rather sizable individuals.

—

A bay window with (left to right) Begonia maculata *var.* wightii *'Swan Song'*, Impatiens *'New Guinea Pink' (foreground), a cattleya hybrid,* Begonia *'Sophie Cecile',* Streptocarpus *'John Innes Marie', and* Trachelospermum asiaticum.

There's more to an eastern exposure, however, than what meets the eye. Our east windows are the most fragrant alcoves in the house. It seems as though aromatic plants such as jasmines, mitriostigma (African gardenia), citrus, cattleyas, and trachelospermums (Confederate jasmines) prefer to thrive, blossom, and send forth their perfume in the soft eastern light. The gentle rays from the east seem to pull the perfumes from their petals and send them wafting into every nook and cranny. First thing in the morning, there's nothing more delightful than waking up to a room steeped in the essence of a few carefully mingled scents.

Angel-Wing Begonias

You've hit a soft spot here. I could rhapsodize for hours about the virtues of angel-wings—after all, I've spent a dozen years caring for this country's largest collection of begonias. But to put it in a nutshell, I feel that angel-wings are aptly named. Thanks to their ruffly foliage, these begonias look like a flock of cherubim about to take flight. Splashed with speckles, streaked with stripes, the foliage alone is enough to hold anyone spellbound. But then, most angel-wings boast big, colorful blossoms to boot. It's almost too much.

Almost, but not quite. Angel-wings tend to be tasteful rather than gaudy, and that trait saves them from tumbling over the brink of excess. True, some angel-wings have rather outlandish leaves, but the flowers are modestly colored. Other angel-wings produce large, plump umbels of bright flowers, but their foliage is usually sedately patterned. Apparently, there's a code of good conduct for angel-wing begonias. Or perhaps, more plausibly, there's a tradition of restraint among breeders.

Most angel-wings are hybrids. At present, there are hundreds of angel-wings in cultivation, all stemming from a handful of Brazilian cane begonia species with deeply lobed leaves. The prototypical angel-wing was *Begonia aconitifolia*, first introduced in 1892. This tall,

Angel-wing begonias combine flowers and ornamental foliage. Two noteworthy year-round bloomers are Begonia 'Orpha C. Fox' *(left) and* Begonia 'Great Gatsby' *(right).*

rather spindly species has a decidedly finicky disposition but extremely handsome banded, maple-shaped leaves. *Begonia aconitifolia* isn't really windowsill fare—it demands high humidity, and if it doesn't get atmospheric moisture the leaf edges crinkle in a totally unacceptable manner. The species would have slipped into obscurity if it weren't for Eva Kenworthy Gray, a begonia grower from California. In 1926, she spotted a diamond in the rough and began a breeding program using *B. aconitifolia* to parent a group of fancy-leaved bloomers. A Wisconsin housewife by the name of Belva Kusler carried on the work, creating a line of gorgeous feather-leaved begonias accented by immense, luminous floral umbels. Her angel-wings and the subsequent hybrids that followed are perfectly comfortable dwelling in any average east-facing windowsill.

Nowadays, angel-wings have completely overshadowed the plain old cane begonias. Actually, there's no clear-cut definition of what constitutes an angel-wing, and so the plants form a motley crew. Often the leaves have deeply lobed, feathered edges, immediately calling the word *wings* to mind. But sometimes the foliage is slender and sleek. Occasionally the leaves are speckled with silver or pink spots against a darker background, and yet other angel-wings have no markings besides a contrasting burgundy underside. Heights range from diminutive six- to twelve-inch-tall plants such as 'La Paloma' to six-foot skyscrapers such as 'Interlaken'. Fat umbels appear either seasonally or throughout the year in shades of white, pink, red, peach, or blazing orange. The flowers themselves are unisexual, always holding the promise of romance between the males with their fluff of stamens and the females with their corkscrew pistils and expectant seed pouches. When pollinated, those pouches swell and cling for several months while their contents ripen, adding further intrigue to the performance.

Some begonias are a challenge to grow, but not angel-wings. Given a well-lit east window, angel-wings will flourish. They don't need the high humidity that rex begonias demand, and they don't suffer from the mildew problems that blight other begonias. With angel-wings, your greatest challenge is the necessity of constant pruning to keep them shapely.

Like all cane begonias, angel-wings tend to produce tall, fat, woody stems that shed leaves as they gain girth. If left to their own devices, they can easily stretch to four or five feet of naked stem with a few leaves balancing on the tips. But there's no reason why that should happen. The trick is to counteract their wayward tendencies by ruthless and strategic pruning from youth to old age. As soon as a fledgling angel-wing reaches six inches in height, pinch the tip to encourage lateral growth. Within a week or so, you'll notice side shoots popping out, and the begonia will begin its transformation from a leggy cutting to a full bouquet of angelic foliage bedecked by many umbels of blossoms. But you can't rest there. Angel-wings should be pruned ruthlessly at least twice a year, in late summer and again in winter. Make no mistake about it—ruthless means cutting stems right back to a nub. Spare only a few bottom leaves and no more than six inches of stem on a mature plant. Pruning not only enhances the immediate show, it also extends an angel-wing's lifespan: Woody stems are forced to initiate new, tender growth and the plant feels young again.

Of course, there's more to growing angel-wings than merely wielding pruning shears. But in other aspects of their cultivation, begonias prefer benign neglect rather than too much TLC. All begonias hate to be soggy, especially in winter, so apply water only when they're dry. And angel-wings are not big eaters. They benefit from a monthly application of 20-20-20 between April and November, but don't even think of fertilizing in winter, when feeding will encourage fat, woody canes.

Begonias prefer to be pot-bound. In fact, angel-wings are happiest when they're growing with three to four feet of verdure aloft sprouting from a five-inch pot. Their toes might seem uncomfortably cramped, but the small accommodations keep the roots well drained. When repotting is absolutely necessary, perform the chore in late winter, spring, or summer—never repot a begonia in fall or early winter when these plants rest. Use a slightly heavier, more fertile medium than you might enlist for most other begonias. Clay pots will provide ballast for the heavy growth above while aiding drainage below.

Mealybugs are the only insect to bother begonias, but they attack angel-wings only as a last resort. Under very damp, closely packed conditions, angel-wings might succumb to fungal infections. To avoid this, provide plenty of space between plants, good air circulation, and don't dampen the foliage on a dreary day.

After years of hanging around angel-wings, I can't help choosing favorites. If asked to recommend the best year-round bloomers, I would turn unhesitatingly to 'Pinafore', a frilly-leaved, salmon-flowered hybrid bred by my father-in-law; 'Tom Ment I', with silver-speckled coppery leaves and matching salmon flowers; 'Orange

Rubra', with modest pale-green leaves but show-stopping carrot-orange floral umbels that emit a honeysuckle fragrance; and 'Orpha C. Fox', notable for her bronze and burgundy leaves splashed with silver and accented by frequent bright-pink blossoms. Those are my favorites today, but no doubt another ravishing angel-wing will catch my eye and steal my soul tomorrow.

Bulbs

Every year in late summer I swear that I won't bother with bulbs. After all, even without them, the windowsill holds plenty of botanical interest throughout the seasons. Yet every year in early winter I find myself stuffing daffodil, freesia, hyacinth, and narcissus bulbs frantically into pots. When March rolls around, every sill in the place is crammed with blooming bulbs of all descriptions. The display might be brief, but it gives me great pleasure, because there's something magical about bulbs that makes them worth all the trouble.

When promoting bulbs, nurserymen like to claim that forced bulbs need no light whatsoever. It's true, to a certain extent—paperwhites, tulips, and other springtime performers will emerge and form buds with very little light. But their flower stalks run up and become spindly when light levels are low. I take the opposite path and give bulbs as much light as I can muster while the flowers develop. In midwinter, the morning rays that rush through east-facing windows are the most brilliant sunbeams of the day. So that's where the bulbs are set.

But I'm getting ahead of myself. First the bulbs must be planted. Although certain compact cultivars are recommended for forcing, I've found that any bulb can be forced in a pot. Since I always seem to purchase flowering bulbs at the eleventh hour, my pots are filled with anything I can lay hands on. In addition to the traditional fare of paperwhites, tulips, and hyacinths, other springtime bulbs such as grape hyacinths, crocuses, dwarf irises, anemones, and lily of the valley work nicely in pots. The whole idea is to simulate spring. Even

⌒

Surely one of winter's greatest pleasures is to revel in the splendor of forced bulbs, such as this windowbox of Narcissus *'February Gold'.*

though these plants might represent just a small fraction of the blooming extravaganza soon to come outdoors, a tiny container filled with a bunch of tulips is ten times more precious in midwinter than an ocean of the same flower performing in the peak of spring.

I prefer to use shallow ornamental clay pots for my bulb-forcing endeavors. After all, several long weeks are spent contemplating a rather lackluster crop of green sprigs, so it helps if the containers are pleasant to behold. No matter what I'm growing, the bulbs are snuggled close together. They are placed growing end up and covered with just enough soil so that the tip skims the surface. Although you don't need good soil to force bulbs (in fact, forcing kits often furnish only pebbles or perlite), mine are cemented in with the same heavy potting medium (equal parts compost, sand, and peat) that I use for geraniums. I figure that a little extra oomph underfoot doesn't hurt. Then the bulbs are shoved under a bench in a near-freezing side porch, which never falls below 36 degrees Fahrenheit and rarely climbs above 45 degrees all winter.

Because winter is long and dull, I check the progress of my forced bulbs several times a week. Although they scarcely need water until signs of life break the soil surface, I can never resist wetting the soil once in a while to speed things along. It makes me feel useful and it does no harm. As soon as growth emerges, the pots are whisked into a cool east window—the cooler, the better. Ours happens to be a bay window set off from the rest of the room, so it remains about 60 degrees Fahrenheit during the day and 50 degrees at night, which suits the bulbs nicely.

That's all there is to it. Water your bulbs when they seem slightly dry—they perform best when grown on the damp side. Although bulb dealers assure us that fertilizing isn't necessary, I give them some nourishment with a weak solution of 20-20-20 when they first go into the window. From then on, they're on their own. The only challenge to forcing bulbs comes when it's time to compose your midwinter display of spring beauties. And that's one of the most pleasant tasks any gardener can ever hope to face. With very little effort, you get a slam-bang show. Somehow, bulb colors seem more brilliant

—

Half the beauty of indoor bulbs comes from growing them in intriguing containers. Here two terra-cotta pots hold Narcissus *'Spellbinder' (left) and a double pink hyacinth. Both perform year after year.*

when they're sitting at your elbow on the windowsill. Cute little crocus look cuter than ever, aromatic daffodils spew forth twice their usual perfume. Even tulips last longer when they're protected from the elements. And the display is wonderfully fluid. You can switch things according to momentary whims, combining shades and juggling the architecture of stems and stalks to your heart's content.

Anybody can do it. Even the clumsiest nongardener in our midst can manage to force bulbs. Of course, when blossoms emerge, there's no feeling of achievement or triumph against stiff odds. And yet, a crop of flowering bulbs silhouetted against frosty windowpanes is one of this world's most fulfilling images. Sometimes, beauty is its own reward.

Cattleyas

Sure, cattleyas are gorgeous and come in a dazzling array of colors and fragrances. But most people have an ulterior motive for growing them: A cattleya in the windowsill is a medal of achievement. It declares to anyone who might be passing by that the gardener in residence has reached a high level of horticultural proficiency.

Actually, cattleyas aren't difficult, they're just different. Everything you've learned about growing other plants must be thrown out the window—cattleyas follow their own set of rules. Mastering the program requires an initial investment of time as you learn the ropes, but eventually, cattleyas require less fuss and bother than most of the other plants in residence. Before long, you'll be growing and flowering cattleyas with the greatest ease.

Even among orchids, cattleyas are a step above the easier and more readily available phalaenopsis, or moth orchids, that have become windowsill standards. Blame it on their native diversity: There are forty-five species of cattleyas hailing from South American habitats ranging from chilly mountainsides to sweltering Amazon jungles. So

An east-facing window provides enough sun for a cattleya hybrid and Impatiens *'Double Amethyst'.*

it stands to reason that the rules for their cultivation are not clearly defined. The game is tricky, but the rewards are great. Watching a cattleya's buds swell is tantamount to reading a good, long suspense thriller. But there's no peeking ahead, and you're personally involved in the plot.

When I speak of diversity, I'm not exaggerating. Bifoliate cattleyas send out clusters of many small blossoms tucked tightly together, while their unifoliate counterparts are crowned by just a few blooms that spread their huge, frilly petals fully six inches wide. The color range is incredible. There isn't a shade missing from the cattleya's spectrum, and those hues are rarely wishy-washy. Forget the insipid mauve orchids that were gingerly pinned to prom gowns when Big Bands were in. Vibrant orange, eye-splitting mustard, lush lavender, and deep magenta are among the rainbow hues that accent cattleya petals now. Nowadays, cattleyas have mingled with other orchids— laelias, brassavolas, sophronitis, and other kindred spirits—to expand the color range and parent more compact, windowsill-size progeny. The new generation is more dramatic in form, with clear-cut lines and strongly defined velvety-petaled blossoms. Contrasting lips are commonplace; often they are also streaked and intricately patterned— tiger spots, zebra stripes, bird's-egg speckling, and every other gimmick in the book come into play. Furthermore, while admiring the floral colors, you're likely to catch a whiff of an incredible perfume wafting from those handsome petals. Not all cattleyas are scented, but those that are so endowed often emit wonderful, full-bodied scents. The essence of cattleya frequently has a fruity tang, although occasionally it speaks with a deep, floral throat or a slightly antiseptic resonance. And this dazzling display can occur at any time of year depending upon the lineage of the cattleya in question. Each cattleya keeps its own schedule, although spring and fall are the seasons of choice for most species and hybrids.

As is no doubt clear by now, it's a cattleya's blossoms that steal the show. In fact, it's a good thing that we are distracted below the neck, because beneath those proud floral stalks are some rather pitiful pale-green leaves that poke at odd angles. I always feel apologetic when it comes to cattleya foliage, but I shouldn't really make excuses because, in cattleya terms, yellowish, sparse leaves signify that everything is going fine. If the foliage is a deep, gorgeous, lush green, then you should begin to worry. It's a delicate balance. If the leaves look

In addition to stunning colors, many cattleya hybrids also emit a delicious scent.

too yellow and sad or if the pseudobulbs begin to shrivel, then the cattleya is receiving too much light. If the leaves are succulent and a dark-green color, they've probably been overfertilized or kept in too dark a spot. The torpid growth might look lush but it's likely to collapse, and you'll never see flowers.

If cattleyas break all the rules, it's because they are epiphytes. In nature, they cling to the top of jungle trees. As a result, a cattleya's wandering, caterpillar-thick roots need abundant drainage and air to survive, while the foliage prefers 50 percent relative humidity. It's possible to provide those conditions in the windowsill by misting the foliage regularly, watering sparsely, and anchoring the roots in coarse fir bark.

The potting medium is crucial. We start our fledgling cattleyas in sphagnum moss and then move them to loosely packed fir bark as soon as they graduate into five-inch pots. Since the growing medium differs from the norm, your watering schedule must change accordingly. It's difficult to discern when a cattleya is dry, because the rigid foliage never wilts. But the pseudobulbs—those plump, swollen parts at the base of the leaves—will shrivel if the plant receives insufficient water. Each year a cattleya makes new growth from which the flower stalk will eventually emerge. Watch that growth and its pseudobulb carefully—it will reveal the first symptoms of distress under adverse conditions. In summer, a cattleya grown in bark usually needs water three times a week. In winter, once a week will suffice. But keep an eye on the pseudobulb. If it wrinkles, decrease the drinks. Water on the morning of a sunny day and bring the plant to the sink or bathtub to give it a generous drenching, wetting foliage and all.

Since fir bark is almost devoid of nutrients, cattleyas must be fertilized regularly. Again, it's a delicate balance. We mix a weak solution of one-quarter teaspoon of 20-20-20 to a gallon of water and apply it once a week while the cattleya is in active growth. When it rests, we withhold food completely.

Repotting cattleyas is a messy operation as you try to wedge bark between the roots without causing too much havoc. Plastic containers can be used, but they tend to topple from the weighty foliage, dumping all those carefully wedged bark pieces unceremoniously on the floor. Although you don't want everyone's attention to leave the eye-riveting flowers and rove downward to the unappetizing leaves, heavy antique terra-cotta pots put ballast below. Repotting should be done only following a resting period when new growth begins. And don't fret about those roots that make no pretense of plunging into the medium but grope into space instead. If they're plump and white, the plant is healthy; there's no need to tuck them in.

Although experts can alter their cattleya's blooming cycle by raising or lowering the thermostat, this is a tricky business. Rather than fiddling with nature, we keep our cattleyas comfortable with a nighttime temperature of 60 degrees Fahrenheit. During the day, the temperature can climb as high as it desires as long as the relative humidity remains at 50 percent.

Although cattleyas look pretty pathetic when they're not in flower, they really don't monopolize much room during the off season. And no matter how pitiful they seem when not performing, they're forgiven when flowers appear. They loom large and last long, declaring your proficiency for all the world to see. And the windowsill is the perfect stage to tout your expertise. Not everyone can flower a cattleya.

Citrus

Most houseplants provide a harvest of blossoms, but citrus yield fruit as well. There's something about a tree dangling with homegrown fruit that causes one's chest to swell with pride. In fact, the seduction of citrus is so strong that you can scarcely dissuade gardeners from trying to grow those golden fruits indoors. As soon as gardeners graduate beyond the basic spider plants and philodendrons, chances are they'll turn their newly green thumbs toward citrus.

Citrus have a lengthy tradition as houseplants. Long before those sun-kissed fruit could be purchased at every corner store, gardeners grew citrus indoors. In Victorian times, a citrus could be found on nearly every sill—at least that was the claim printed in several magazines of the period. Actually, chilly nineteenth-century homes provided the perfect environment for growing citrus trees, slipping down to 50 degrees Fahrenheit at night. In addition, Victorian homes furnished another primary requirement: large windows, giving those sizable plants a wide arena of eastern rays.

Citrus are bulky bushes. Customers often ask if we stock dwarf citrus trees. Well, any citrus will stay dwarf when its roots are confined in a pot. Still, a mature citrus will eventually sink its toes into a twelve- to fourteen-inch pot while its branches will monopolize three to four square feet of window space. This makes citrus perfect for picture windows or sunporches.

All citrus have fragrant flowers, and the perfume is heavenly. Although noses differ greatly on their floral preferences, citrus exude a scent that anyone can love. Most citrus open their white, waxy blossoms in profusion both summer and winter. If fruit is your goal, a little dusting around with a small paintbrush will ensure pollination and increase the crop.

Since all citrus are roughly the same size and the blossoms are

equally aromatic, you can let your tastebuds dictate your selection. Oranges and lemons top the most-wanted list. If it's oranges you're after, I would suggest either *Citrus sinensis* 'Valencia' or the navel orange, *C. s.* 'Washington', for windowsill growing. The best lemon to keep the pantry stocked is *C. limon* 'Meyer'. However, if you have a flair for the fantastic, by all means grow the ponderosa lemon (*C. l.* 'Ponderosa') for its gigantic five-pound fruit. That's not a misprint: Ponderosa lemons are immense—bigger than any grapefruit I've encountered. Those oversize lemons aren't really of supermarket quality because of their thick rind and pithy texture. But once you've squeezed the juice (and there's plenty of juice to extract), it tastes just as tart as any other lemon on the market. And thanks to that thick rind, ponderosas last for months in the refrigerator. Still, a ponderosa's impact is primarily visual—they certainly raise eyebrows.

Beyond lemons and oranges, there are plenty of novelty citrus worthy of residence on the windowsill. You might want to cultivate a taste for tangerines, in which case try *C. reticulata* 'Dancy'. If limes tingle your tastebuds, try *C. aurantiifolia* 'Persian Lime' (also known as the Bearss lime or the Tahitian lime) or *C. a.* 'Key Lime', which has tiny leaves and small but intensely aromatic fruit. If you want to get the biggest harvest per square foot of window space, the kumquat is by far the best choice. The sweetest kumquat is *Fortunella margarita* 'Meiwa'. It yields a bounty of thumb-size, sugary fruit that rarely make it to the table—they're usually popped into the mouth, rind and all. After an initial pucker, the aftertaste is scrumptious. Unfortunately, I have yet to find a grapefruit suited to life on the sill.

Having selected a citrus, all you need to do is grow the plants to fruiting size. The wait for fruit will be quite a bit shorter if you start with a cutting or graft from a mature citrus rather than planting seeds. Seedlings can take up to thirteen years to flower and set fruit, although some kumquats will fruit in a mere seven years from seed. Moreover, if you plant seeds of a 'Valencia' orange, the fruit probably won't even turn out to be a true 'Valencia' after all your patience. A cutting from a fruiting citrus should blossom shortly after roots are

Although not directly sitting in the window, ×Citrofortunella mitis 'Variegata' (left), Impatiens *'Double Salmon' (right), and* Columnea *'Campfire' (below) bask in the sunbeams rushing through an east-facing door.*

formed and new growth begins. As soon as your fledgling is large enough to support the weight, fruit should successfully set and ripen. The same is true for grafts, although the grafting process itself takes several months.

Meanwhile, you are the indoor orchardist. Growing citrus is not simple, although the basics are easy enough: Grow citrus in an east or south window, water them when dry, and give them nighttime temperatures of 55 degrees Fahrenheit. Pruning is not a frequent chore, but a few strategic snips will send branches shooting in the desired direction.

Beyond the basics, citrus suffer from several nutritional problems. Citrus have a galloping appetite, especially for potassium. In fact, Victorian gardeners frequently scratched wood ash into the soil to provide a quick shot of this nutrient. Although it's not too difficult to keep abreast of a citrus's needs for potassium, or for the other major nutrients (nitrogen and phosphorous), their hunger for micronutrients can prove befuddling. In containers, citrus often experience iron, zinc, and manganese deficiencies. A watchful eye on the foliage will detect the first telltale signs of a micronutrient deficiency before any serious harm befalls the plant. If the leaves turn yellow with pea-green veining, you can safely suspect that more iron is needed. If the leaves turn bright yellow with very dark-green veins, zinc might be lacking from the plant's diet. And if the foliage turns pale overall with reduced fruit production, a manganese deficiency is probably the culprit. All three deficiencies can be rapidly cured by a foliar spray of iron, zinc, or manganese chelate. However, when temperatures are too chilly, the micronutrients sometimes aren't absorbed. If supplemental spraying brings no tangible results, simply bring the plant into a warmer spot.

In general, citrus should be fertilized with 20-20-20 or any other balanced fertilizer once a month. In autumn, it's wise to apply a foliar spray of micronutrients to get the jump on deficiencies. In winter, fertilizing citrus can be tricky. Decrease the frequency and dilution of feedings while keeping an eagle eye on the foliage. Citrus sometimes suffer from toxicity problems in winter if fertilizer salts accumulate. If this is the case, you'll notice browning leaf edges and a sickly cast throughout the rest of the leaf. The cure is a grueling leaching process wherein you drench the soil several times. It's tough medicine for a citrus to endure and occasionally you'll lose a plant to the cure. Moderation in fertilizing at the onset is a much better idea.

The fruit of ×Citrofortunella microcarpa *is rather tart to the taste but makes excellent marmalade*

Citrus wilt easily when new growth sprouts in spring, and so watering should be more frequent during this season. At other times of year, water frugally—soggy roots can disrupt nutrient absorption and invite all sorts of disease problems.

Once you've worked out their diet, you're home free. Citrus aren't plagued by many pests indoors. Scale and mealybugs are the most common foe. Aphids reputedly torment citrus, but we've never witnessed an infestation. Victorian gardeners subjected their citrus to frequent and brisk soap-and-water baths as preventative medicine. In my opinion, bathing remains a simple and effective means of washing problems away.

The rewards of your efforts taste very juicy indeed. But if you'd rather leave the evidence of your expertise dangling on the bush for all the world to see, go right ahead. Oranges cling to their branches for several months, often shriveling and going sour before letting go, but lemons tumble to the ground as soon as they're fully ripe. No matter how long the ripe fruit remains on the stem, the immature fruits of most citrus spend half a year gradually turning from leprechaun green to their ripe color. So you've got plenty of time to admire your handiwork and plan the menu. Of all the plants on the windowsill, not only are citrus the most mouthwatering, they're the most fulfilling as well.

Clivias

Clivias are almost too good to be true. Just when everyone is deeply entrenched in wintertime doldrums, clivias come to the rescue. We spend the beginning of the season anticipating the flowers and the worst part of winter immersed in their fiery blossoms. Not many plants make such spectacular use of low light.

Clivias are handsome at any time of year. As you might guess from their straplike leaves, their season of bloom, and those gaping blossoms, clivias are members of the amaryllis family. But clivias go one step further. On a well-grown clivia, the broad, flat foliage is neatly stacked on either side of a central growing tip, every leaf in place like a deftly arranged bouffant. When mature, clivias stand two to three feet tall, while their gracefully arching leaves spread into an equally wide wingspan. Granted, they monopolize a generous chunk of window room, but the space is well used, whether blossoms are present or not. And when flower stalks begin to jut out from the center of the neatly parted leaves, everyone is held spellbound until the buds finally show color. Not a bad way to spend winter.

A few misunderstandings plague clivias. First of all, it's high time gardeners began to pronounce the name correctly. It's CLY-vee-ah, and they were introduced from South Africa in 1823 and named in honor of Lady Charlotte Florentina Clive, Duchess of Northumberland. Although clivias are frequently promoted as favorite Victorian plants, that claim stretches the truth. Until the early part of this century, *Clivia nobilis*, a species with dense umbels but relatively small

Clivia miniata *clad in its umbels of late-season spring flowers.*

Collectors make a business of seeking out Clivia miniata *hybrids with slight variations of flower color.*

and comparatively dull buff-colored flowers, was the only clivia in cultivation. And it certainly didn't reside in every home. Far from it.

It wasn't until the middle of the twentieth century that *C. miniata* happened upon the scene and stole the show. Native to Natal, this bulbous plant was given the nickname of Kaffir lily early in the game. (You won't find me using that common name, however; the word has unpleasant racial connotations, and there's no reason why horticulture should be sullied by ethnic slurs.) Even in its original, unhybridized state, *C. miniata* bears spectacular blossoms. Each bell-shaped flower is colored salmon to orange and enhanced by a striking yellow eye.

To add to the intrigue, there's a lot of diversity from plant to plant. Some clivias send their flower scapes towering a foot or more above the foliage; others nestle their buds into the crevice of the leaves and the flowers open with chins just above the foliage. Some clivias have airy, loose-petaled blossoms; others are nearly gapless. You can select a clivia according to your heart's desire.

In addition to this natural diversity, hybridizers have tinkered with the blossom colors. Quite a few years ago, the American market was captured by Belgian hybrids with deeper orange petals and fatter umbels. More recently, a South African firm claimed to have developed a cultivar bearing screaming-red flowers. We fell for it, but so far the flowers haven't lived up to their billing. At the moment, the Rolls Royce among clivias is the yellow *C. m.* 'Aurea' (sometimes called 'Citrina' or 'Flava'). No doubt you've heard of it. Just between you and me, the light lemon-yellow flowers of 'Aurea' aren't half as showy as the orange version. But you can't tell that to collectors willing to plunk down hundreds (sometimes thousands) of dollars for a yellow clivia. Beauty has nothing to do with it. 'Aurea' is pricey because there are only a few dozen plants in the United States and everyone wants to boast of a thoroughbred in their stable. Rarer still is *C. m.* 'Striata' with cream streaks running down its leaves and shy orange blossoms. At this writing, less than half a dozen variegated clivias inhabit the United States, and unless you are on intimate terms with a clivia specialist, your chances of obtaining one are virtually nil. Furthermore, they grow so slowly and form divisions so infrequently that the supply is not likely to increase soon.

Even excluding the exorbitantly priced yellow and variegated cultivars, clivias are costly compared to run-of-the-mill houseplants. Perhaps that explains why we receive several phone calls a week from indoor gardeners concerned about the health and welfare of their plants. Actually, they shouldn't fret. Clivias are close to unkillable. They'll tolerate quite a lot of abuse, but a few hints might help coax forth those stupendous flowers.

Seedlings usually need to be three years old before they settle into the serious business of producing blossoms. When they've reached that ripe age, autumn is the time to prepare for their winter display. For a month to six weeks from October to November, water very moderately (let the soil go almost, but not quite, to the parching point), withhold fertilizer completely, and don't repot. Nighttime temperatures should slip down to 45 to 55 degrees Fahrenheit. This autumnal resting period is crucial. Meanwhile, the foliage shouldn't show the slightest hint that the plant is resting—not a shrivel or a brown streak anywhere to mar the clivia's immaculate image. In late November, you can resume watering again. Feed once every three to four weeks when buds appear.

It's best to grow clivias in clay pots to provide ballast for the top-heavy foliage. But don't use your favorite antique terra-cotta pot. The roots are so plump and aggressive that they often break their container. Paradoxically, these plants blossom best when pot-bound. If they don't burst their seams, clivias can remain in the same container for years. When repotting, use a heavy, sandy soil.

One good excuse to repot a clivia is to divide offsets from the mother plant, although there's nothing wrong with letting offsets stay on their parent indefinitely. Young divisions don't fare well on their own, so wait until an offset is nearly as large as the mother plant before separating it. When the time comes, dividing a clivia is no easy feat. If you can, enlist someone with plenty of muscle and patience to perform the chore and then stand at their elbow fretting while they delicately unravel the interwoven root mass. A clivia's thick, wormlike roots are extremely brittle and break easily if the task is done clumsily. Attempt the deed only for very dear friends or to acquire something quite rare in exchange.

Another method of sharing clivias is to plant seed. Clivias set seed easily, but a year will elapse while the green fruit ripens to red and is ready for sowing. Then several years go by before flowers appear. Obviously, clivias are not for impatient gardeners, but they look just fine along the way. For all their majesty, clivias require very little care. Except during the autumnal chilling period, nighttime temperatures can fall into the forties or rise into the sixties—clivias don't mind. (When they are grown in a very warm environment in winter, however, they sometimes send out blossoms off-season rather than producing much-needed wintertime flowers.) Likewise, these bulbs don't demand high humidity. If a room is very dry, the leaf edges will brown, but your lips will probably become painfully chapped long before the clivia begins to protest.

Clivias give houseplants a good name. They have the sort of sophistication that houseplants rarely muster, which makes them a pleasure to display. Clivias do an east window proud.

Gesneriads

I grew up among African violets. Every morning when I awoke and groped my way to the kitchen for breakfast, African violets greeted me. There they were, lined up along the counter, a row of little bloomers each set on its own saucer. My mother would come in and pop the bread in the toaster with one hand while wielding her copper watering can and filling the saucers with the other. Those violets may not have been terribly exciting, but they provided a reliable display for a much-used and heavily heated but not overly sunlit room.

Although there's a special spot in my heart for African violets, I wouldn't choose to harbor those mastheads of the family Gesneriaceae on my own windowsill. I like to think that I've graduated to more challenging gesneriads. And to tell the truth, at the moment African violets are passé. Likewise, the closely related gloxinias are not strong contenders on the market. Yet the gesneriad family is definitely well represented in east-facing windows throughout the land, for other family members have stepped in to fill the gap. Although these newcomers might not blossom with the same stubborn persistence as their dowdier relatives, their seasonal show is more spectacular.

Right now, streptocarpus are all the rage. Nearly as easy to grow as African violets, they blossom most of the year, their flowers are profuse, and they come in a broad spectrum of colors including white, pinks, blues, purples, and reds. Streptocarpus form a rosette of long, velvety, heavily textured leaves surrounding a little bouquet of tubular blossoms held on short stems. They look for all the world like primroses, but you can admire their charms throughout the year. In fact, they are commonly known as Cape primroses, and their wildling look has helped them escape the frumpy associations that plague African violets.

Streptocarpellas are just a stone's throw from streptocarpus genetically and are often mentioned in the same breath. But unlike streptocarpus, streptocarpellas are upright, branching plants with thumbnail-size leaves and multitudes of blossoms in shades of lilac and purple. *Streptocarpella saxorum*, a species from Kenya and Tasmania, was everyone's heartthrob until it was superseded by its offspring, the everblooming 'Good Hope' with inch-wide clear purple blossoms, and 'Sparkle' with wine-purple blooms. Streptocarpellas prefer to dangle in hanging containers that they eventually surround in wiry stems and airy blossoms.

Of all the gesneriads, I'm particularly partial to columneas. Apparently, plenty of other gardeners share my proclivity. Most columneas are trailers, sending trains of small-leaved branches showering from the pot. Even without pruning, columneas are invariably well clad. In autumn, they begin the serious business of producing quantities of buds. And from that moment until spring, the foliage is hidden behind dragonshead blossoms in fiery shades of yellow, orange, and deep red. Did I say dragonshead? If you use your imagination, these gaping blooms look delightfully like ferocious mini-monsters about to breathe fumes. (Kids love them.) Some flowers are covered with a soft down; others sport domed hoods and tufted ears. With 160 species and countless hybrids in cultivation, there's plenty of diversity to keep collectors transfixed.

Aeschynanthus—known as lipstick plants—will also begin in autumn to form floral bracts for their winter show. In a family that generally demands high humidity but abhors moist toes, aeschynanthus can tolerate quite a bit of abuse. Of all the gesneriads, they are best suited for beginners. Their waxy foliage is impervious to water and light damage, and always looks impeccable. But it's not the hoya-like leaves that most gardeners covet. Aeschynanthus start their display with equally waxy, deep-red or sometimes darkest-burgundy floral bracts, which could easily satisfy anyone's desire for a colorful show. But there's more. By the time holiday season rolls around, bright red trumpets begin to peer from the center of those darker bells. Considering their nifty red-and-green outfit and their blooming time, I'm surprised lipstick plants haven't been enlisted as alternatives to poinsettias. I suspect that the reason lies with the dangling foliage, which might be difficult for mass marketers to transport.

I could go on and fill several more pages with juicy descriptions, but there are simply too many window-worthy gesneriads to describe at length. However, some notables that merit closer attention include the sinningias, especially the tiniest micromidget types that can fit

—

Plants and their sculpture can become an art form. A loose wreath of Jasminum mesnyi *is in full flower in late winter, flanked by the gesneriads* Aeschynanthus hildebrandii *(left) and* Codonanthe *'Aurora'.*

Known as flame violets, episcias usually blossom in shades of bright scarlet, with the exception of Episcia 'Pink Panther', *shown here.*

easily in a thimble; episcias, or flame violets, with plush leaves over-laid with brocadelike patterns; nematanthus, with bloated orange blossoms that look like a school of tiny goldfish; kohlerias, which produce soft leaves on tall upright stems lined by intricately marked orangish-red blossoms; and the bulbous achimenes, which blossom in vibrant shades for a brief time during the warm season.

Although gesneriads form a diverse group, their cultural require-ments are very similar. Early in my gardening career, I learned that these members of the African violet family all prefer to be watered from below. My mother's morning ritual remained firmly in my mind until the moment that I, too, had to tackle the care and watering of gesneriads. I soon discovered that it's not the direction the water comes from that matters, it's that gesneriads vehemently detest water-splashed leaves. Most gesneriad leaves will stain if a stray droplet falls on their surface and is not dried off immediately. As if that weren't enough, drinks must also be served lukewarm. Fortunately, gesneriads prefer to go slightly thirsty, so you won't have to fret about their watering crotchets too frequently.

After you've catered to watering whims, there's not much else to challenge your expertise. All members of the gesneriad family prefer to sink their toes into a light, peaty growing medium. Most garden centers conveniently sell a soil specifically mixed for African violets and their kin. Pack it lightly around the roots, leaving plenty of air pockets. But repotting shouldn't be a frequent chore—gesneriads prefer to be pot-bound. You're likely to overwater a generously potted plant, and that's a cardinal sin from a gesneriad's viewpoint.

Moderation is the watchword for gesneriads, and that goes for feeding as well. Fertilizing once every four to six weeks throughout the year will suffice if the plant is grown in a loamy medium rather than a soilless mix. Use a balanced fertilizer such as 20-20-20, and never splatter fertilizer-tinged water on those sensitive leaves.

Although most residents of an east window can tolerate and will even enjoy a stint in a southern exposure, gesneriads are an exception. Their leaves twist and burn if they receive too much light. Thus, if your east window is heavily sun-drenched during certain hours of the day, move the gesneriads away from direct rays.

All gesneriads demand warm temperatures. If nighttime temperatures dip below 63 degrees Fahrenheit, even for an evening, you're likely to see damage on felt-leaved varieties. But the sky is the limit during the day, as long as the humidity remains between 40 and 50 percent. Don't resort to misting in your efforts to raise the humidity—remember that gesneriads dislike wet leaves.

Gesneriads are prone to cyclamen mites, a microscopic scourge that causes contortions in the new growth. As the infestation worsens, growth ceases altogether. Meanwhile, the little beasts travel from plant to plant with lightning speed. It's wise to discard an infected plant immediately, since it will never look praiseworthy again.

African violets are a wonderful starting point for gardeners taking

In autumn and winter, the yawning blossoms of Columnea 'Evlo' *gape like so many fiery dragons.*

their first steps toward floral profusion. Heaven knows, they set me on the right path. Then, after mastering the easiest members of the family, there's plenty of room for exploration within the clan. Even if you decided to grow only members of Gesneriaceae, your east window would never be dull or flowerless for a single day.

Impatiens

There are moments when even the best gardener on the block yearns for instant gratification. That's why we have impatiens. You can pot up the tiniest impatiens sprig today and see blossoms tomorrow—or at least soon thereafter. And from that point on, until you grow weary of the display, your impatiens will be studded with blossoms. Which explains how they came by that obnoxious common name, busy lizzies.

Even gardeners who pooh-pooh impatiens as too plebeian often relent when other flowers are few and far between. Despite their legendary dependability, impatiens didn't make a big splash on the windowsill until Longwood Gardens, in Kennett Square, Pennsylvania, introduced the first New Guinea hybrids in 1972. Prior to that, the species *Impatiens walleriana* sometimes wandered indoors where it put on a rather straggly but floriferous display. True, *I. walleriana* was always heavily beset with gaudy magenta blossoms, but at the same time the flowers were perched atop half-naked arms and legs, and it shed spent flowers everywhere. Then along came the New Guineas. From a handful of species collected in the Australasian jungles, Longwood Gardens bred a series of plants with incredibly lush flower colors, compact habits, and sometimes ornamental leaves as well. The rest is history.

I'm sure you've met New Guinea hybrid impatiens somewhere in your travels—they're omnipresent. If you see one- to two-foot-tall impatiens forming a perfect mound of two-inch-long, slender leaves, totally studded with one- to two-inch-wide, five-petaled blossoms, it is undoubtedly a New Guinea hybrid. Longwood Gardens named its series for the circus, with such notables as pink-and-white-streaked 'Fortune Teller', deep-pink 'Juggler', cherry-red 'Cannonball', salmon 'Trapeze', and snow-white 'Ringmaster'. Other hybridizers entered the act, expanded the color range, and gave their introductions equally imaginative names such as 'Star Wars', 'Telstar', and 'Orbiter'. Nowadays, New Guinea impatiens can be purchased in the supermarket under generic names, and they're just as good (if not better) than the original series. Just select your favorite hue.

After the New Guinea hybrids broke the ice, other impatiens rode in on their coattails. In the 1980s, just when the New Guinea fad began to cool, a group of miniature impatiens appeared on the market to rekindle the flames. Although New Guineas demand plenty of space on the sill, the new miniatures are quite modest. Named for the Hawaiian Islands, these impatiens stand only a foot tall at maturity and are continually smothered in tiny, dime-size blossoms, each with a pronounced spur. So far, we have only a handful of hybrids, all in shades of pink, but the color range is bound to expand.

If the miniatures turned a few heads, the next innovation on the impatiens scene—double rosebud impatiens—definitely stole much of the New Guinea hybrids' thunder. Standing the same height as New Guineas, the doubles have smaller, oval leaves hidden behind profuse, fluffy blossoms. The first double was the pearly 'White Gardenia', with two-inch-wide, many-petaled flowers. It performed with such tireless vigor and became such an immediate success that breeders hustled to introduce a slew of other hybrids dappled with small pom-poms of peach, pink, amethyst, or red.

For tastes that run toward the bizarre, impatiens have their share of strange relatives. *Impatiens niamniamensis* 'Congo Cockatoo' is a tropical African hybrid with sparsely clad, pencil-straight stems surrounded by cornucopia-shaped blossoms colored just like candy corn. Along the same lines, 'African King' has broad, burgundy-backed, fluted leaves and matching maroon cornucopia blossoms hugging the stems. If a trailer is needed, *I. repens* from Sri Lanka fills the bill, with roaming, succulent pink stems and masses of tiny, maidenhair-size leaves. Occasionally, in the heat of summer, a lurid yellow, snail-shaped blossom will open, but it's not a frequent occurrence—*I. repens* is primarily a foliage plant.

All impatiens are easy to grow. A slam-bang display is so simple to achieve that they pose no challenge to a gardener's talents whatsoever. But not all gardeners want to be challenged, and others are so busy being challenged elsewhere that they welcome a chance to sit back and enjoy free entertainment. The only chore that impatiens require is unfailing visits with the watering can. Impatiens are such thirsty plants that they'll faint into a dead wilt with startling rapidity. In summer, be prepared to water an impatiens both morning and early afternoon. If you're an hour late, expect to find them lying in a swoon. Fortunately, it's usually just an act. The succulent stems revive just as rapidly as they collapse. However, forget to water an impatiens for more than a day in midsummer, and you'll find a death scene beyond all hope of resuscitation.

—

A blushing pink arrangement of Impatiens *'Hawaiian Pink' (left),* Impatiens *'Double Amethyst', and* Streptocarpus *'Light Pink' (right foreground).*

There are ways around the watering problem. Grow impatiens in generously large containers and root prune when further promotions are impossible. Sit the pot in a saucer of water in summer and keep the leaves shielded from any direct sunrays. If the air is dry, mist the leaves or sprinkle them with water droplets.

Impatiens also have a hearty appetite. They prefer a heavy, nourishing soil underfoot and feedings every two to three weeks. To keep an impatiens expanding in girth rather than height, prune drastically once every two to three months. New growth will sprout in a week. Not long thereafter, the plant will look like a million dollars again.

Impatiens are prone to aphids, mealybugs, red spider mites, and cyclamen mites. The first symptoms of cyclamen mites on impatiens are curling of the new growth and contorted, sickle-shaped leaves. Cut back the infected plant ruthlessly, release predatory mites to clean up leftover cyclamen mites, and keep the plant quarantined until the new growth shows no signs of damage. To combat the other pests, check "Houseplant Care" (page 197).

You can grow a prizewinning impatiens in record time. Busy lizzies become boast-worthy plants without burdening your green thumb. And there's no reason why all your horticultural achievements must be hard won. In no time flat, you'll be basking in more blossoms than you ever dreamed possible while scarcely lifting a finger. Sometimes, botany should be blissfully simple.

Jasmines

People who scarcely show the slightest interest in growing houseplants nonetheless adopt a jasmine. After all, there's something alluring about cultivating your own little perfume dispenser. And thanks to the pleasing disposition of most jasmines, new converts usually enjoy success. Jasmines have baited and hooked many budding houseplant enthusiasts.

The double impatiens, with their constant supply of rosebud-shaped flowers, are all the rage and new colors, such as Impatiens *'Double Amethyst', appear regularly.*

Jasmines should be grown close by. When sunrays are magnified through windowpanes, they intensify the flowers' aroma. The uncorked perfume has nowhere to wander but straight into your awaiting nostrils. Fortunately, most jasmines emit the sort of scent that any nose can live with intimately. During the day, jasmines tinge the air with a pleasant but barely perceptible perfume. At night, that aroma adds sweet overtones and floats even further afield. Nothing could be nicer.

Since jasmines put out such an oversize scent, everyone expects the flowers to be equally bold. In truth, most jasmines have relatively modest blossoms. They are generally star-shaped, less than an inch in diameter, and white. Yellow and pink jasmines might be pleasant to look at, but they lack the deep scent of their pure white counterparts. And somehow a jasmine just isn't worth considering indoors if it lacks a notable aroma.

There are two hundred jasmines in cultivation and many are fragrant. Even after narrowing our list down to the most aromatic jasmines suitable for windowsills, there are still plenty of choices. Some indoor gardeners select jasmines solely on the basis of a fleeting aromatic memory—of *Jasminum sambac* strung into wedding leis or strewn in Hindu temples, perhaps. But, those people who aren't chasing an olfactory recollection often base their choice on stature rather than smell. They look at their growing space to ascertain whether it can better accommodate a bush or vining jasmine. Whichever they prefer, there are still plenty of possibilities.

People who hail from India and thereabouts often harbor a soft spot for sambac jasmines. Best known among these bush-type jasmines is 'Maid of Orleans', the Arabian tea jasmine otherwise known as *sampaquita*, the national flower of the Philippines. 'Maid of Orleans' is by far the easiest and most rewarding sambac jasmine for a windowsill. Throughout the year, it is seldom without a semidouble blossom or two perching on top of its broad, oval leaves. Those flowers open pure white and last only a day before blushing to burgundy and tumbling to the ground. In fact, a little jostling on opening day will dislodge a blossom and send it to a premature demise, but

Although Jasminum tortuosum *flowers tend to be sparse, the fragrance of several in unison is delightful*

fortunately another bud is always in the offing and the aroma persists even after the blossom is spent. And what an aroma: 'Maid of Orleans' sends forth a heavenly combination of May wine touched by cloves that becomes even more intense at dusk.

There are other tempting sambac jasmines. 'Grand Duke of Tuscany' has oversize, many-petaled blossoms that look for all the world like mums and emit a heady gardenia scent. Judged solely on fragrance, 'Grand Duke of Tuscany' would win hands down, and for that virtue it has received quite a bit of publicity. But it has an awkward, lanky growth habit that is nearly impossible to manage on the windowsill. Unlike 'Maid of Orleans' with its tightly stacked foliage, 'Grand Duke of Tuscany' sends naked whips flailing in the air with flowers at the very tip. Better candidates for windowsill purposes are *J. s.* 'Belle of India' or 'Arabian Nights'. Each has its own variation on sambac's fragrant theme. 'Belle of India' features hose-in-hose white blossoms tinged pink toward the center, while 'Arabian Nights' has snow-white blossoms with a tuft of extra petals that emit an aroma nearly as heady as 'Grand Duke of Tuscany'.

I rank *J. nitidum*, the star or windmill jasmine, right up with the sambacs as far as olfactory virtues and windowsill suitability are concerned. Then why hasn't *J. nitidum* made a hit on the market? It seems to be purely a matter of connections. *Jasminum nitidum* is a relatively recent introduction from the Admiralty Islands, so it lacks the colorful associations that sambacs claim. But the windmill jasmine's day will come. The scent is clean and soapy, like fresh laundry hung out to dry, and the flowers expand into a two-inch-wide aura of thin, pointed, glistening white petals. The scent is delightful, the flowers are handsome, but the foliage is head and shoulders above any other jasmine. Standing no taller than three feet in a pot, *J. nitidum* has deep forest-green, shiny leaves that form a dense network of self-branching stems.

Known as the French perfume jasmine or poet's jasmine, *J. officinale* 'Grandiflorum' exudes an intoxicatingly irresistible aroma. Yet this vining jasmine is not for beginners. The perfume jasmine has an inherent awkwardness that might easily perplex all but seasoned indoor gardeners. What to do with those loose, stretching stems that need support but refuse to grasp a crutch? Obviously, a trellis is in order, but tying the stems in can turn into a full-time job.

When mature and neatly trained, the French perfume jasmine looks

Although Jasminum tortuosum *is a newcomer to the houseplant scene, it's one of the easiest, most floriferous, and most pleasantly aromatic jasmines for indoor growing.*

rather nice studded here and there by loose-petaled blossoms. But even in bloom, maintenance is the key. The star-shaped flowers brown after a few days and must be clipped off, since they refuse to fall.

The French perfume jasmine poses a challenge in more ways than one. From late autumn until midwinter, *J. officinale* 'Grandiflorum' can suffer from leaf die-back that sometimes progresses into an unsightly mess. We're not absolutely sure of the cause, but fertilizing only makes matters worse. At the first hint of shriveled leaf edges, decrease waterings and immediately prune off any stricken parts. When new growth resumes in late winter, you're in the clear.

A much easier alternative is *J. tortuosum*. From a distance, it looks similar to the French perfume jasmine. But the growth has more body, the blossoms are more frequent and borne in larger umbels, and the whole shebang is generally more pleasant to look upon. This South African native doesn't treat your nose badly either—the aroma is soapy with citrus overtones. Best of all, there's no dormant period to contend with.

Although *J. polyanthum* is a relative newcomer to the scene, this fast-moving vine quickly became a superstar. In fact, from Thanksgiving onward, you'll find its likeness splashed all over horticultural newspapers and magazines with the lure, "Blooms in the Dead of Winter," spread underneath. Most folks find that promise irresistible and send for the plant posthaste. Alas, few ever see blossoms. When given very cool temperatures (40 to 50 degrees Fahrenheit) for a month in autumn, *J. polyanthum* obligingly sets buds. And if temperatures remain chilly, those buds will open into white clouds of star-shaped blossoms. The fragrance is immense. It is so strong that some find it cloying, and it travels into every corner of the house. But who keeps their house cold enough to coax forth those effusive flowers? If temperatures are set up at normally comfortable living conditions (i.e., 65 degrees), the buds of *J. polyanthum* disappear long before they swell. Even without the flowers, though, *J. polyanthum* forms a nice network of lacy leaves. If given a late-summer pruning to encourage new growth, an eight-inch hanging container will remain in prime condition for years. But a blossomless jasmine is a tease that most gardeners can scarcely tolerate. I usually steer gardeners toward a more rewarding jasmine instead.

All jasmines will thrive in an east-facing window. Sambac blossoms nonstop throughout the year except for a brief rest in midwinter. You might see some discolored leaves when resting time arrives, but don't panic—the plants always pull out of it as the days lengthen. Although the sambacs and *J. nitidum* are considered to be bush-type jasmines, they can send up wayward winding shoots in the first flush of youthful growth. Just prune those back; subsequent sprouts will be tighter. Vining jasmines should be pruned and wound according to your

space. Jasmines prefer generous root room and they like frequent
feeding—once every three to four weeks with 20–20–20 should do it.
Jasmines are rarely bothered by insects besides the ubiquitous
mealybug.

Granted, choosing among all those jasmines can be mind-boggling.
But sampling and selecting jasmines is one of life's little pleasures.
And living with natural perfume floating directly from the flowers
straight to your nose is a joy only window gardeners can experience.

Mitriostigmas

Not all houseplants grow by leaps and bounds—some progress at
a snail's pace. And yet if you have limited space and plenty of
plants, you might welcome a few lethargic botanicals.

You need never fear that *Mitriostigma axillare* will burst through
the ceiling overnight. In fact, you can pot a mitriostigma into a four-
inch container and rest in the confidence that the chore won't need
to be repeated for several years. And you can snuggle a mitriostigma
close beside other plants without worrying that it will infringe on
their turf. If you prefer predictable plants, mitriostigma is for you.

Nevertheless, *M. axillare* puts on quite a performance in a very
modest space. Commonly called the African gardenia, mitriostigma is
in fact a close cousin of the true gardenias. You might not readily
guess the kinship from the thin, dainty leaves and the relatively de-
mure, arbutuslike white blossoms, but one quick visit with your nostrils reveals the one trait that runs throughout the fraternity. The
scent isn't overwhelming and it doesn't float around with gardenialike
garrulity, but it's quite pleasantly redolent when sampled close-up.
The fragrance could be likened to laid-back gardenia with none of
the musky overtones.

Even if the African gardenia doesn't wow you with its sheer energy,
you will undoubtedly be impressed by its dogged persistence. There's
scarcely a week out of the year when mitriostigma isn't covered with
flowers or dotted with a crop of promising buds. In fact, I've always
suspected that the mitriostigma's slow growth rate might be due to
the fact that this little bush expends all its strength producing blossoms. The flowers come in clusters tucked close to the stem at the

Mitriostigma axillare fills low-light areas with handsome foliage, umbels of flowers, and a heavenly scent.

base of the leaves. At first, a small twig will have only a few flowers. But as an African gardenia matures, all its branches are lined with fragrant blossoms. Each five-petaled, open-faced bloom is half an inch wide, and a glistening white in color with pink highlights. If you can call up a picture of citrus flowers in your mind's eye (citrus is also a member of the family Rubiaceae), you're not far from imagining the subtle charms of a mitriostigma flower.

For convenience, I've cubbyholed the African gardenia with plants that prefer east windows, but it could fit in any section of this book. In a pinch, mitriostigma will tolerate much less light than you generally find pouring through panes facing east. It will thrive and bloom in a west-facing window, and can even survive a northern exposure, although flowers will be sparse or nonexistent. And of course, the African gardenia could also live happily ever after in a southern exposure.

The African gardenia will take all sorts of less than optimal conditions in stride. Although it prefers temperatures that hover around 60 degrees Fahrenheit at night, it will endure much colder or warmer conditions without a whimper. A dry home is not its favorite environment, but I've never encountered leaf edge browning because of low humidity. It prefers to dry out slightly between drinks, but if you forget to water your African gardenia once in a while, that's OK. And if your toddler drenches it sometimes, that's fine too. This plant can fit into any life-style.

Fertilize mitriostigma in a manner befitting a very slow-paced plant. Once every four to six weeks should do it. Actually, you could forget to feed an African gardenia altogether and it would never complain. The foliage will stay dark green and never show the slightest sign of distress.

Considering the plant's slow growth rate, pruning really isn't a major issue. Mitriostigmas branch readily with no encouragement whatsoever. You can prune for shaping if you like, but remember that new growth will not sprout immediately to take up the slack. African gardenias tend to take a certain stance. From the moment it begins to grow, a mitriostigma will shoot straight up or sprawl sideways. No matter how hard you try to coax the plant otherwise, it's locked in for life, stubbornly maintaining its original growth pattern. So, if you plan to train a mitriostigma standard, be sure to select an upright-growing plant at the onset. And remember that your specimen can take many years to attain two feet in height.

As you might expect from a plant with impeccably good manners, mitriostigma is prone to few insects. Aphids will attack the tender growth, but only in a fit of desperation. Scale is a more frequent offender. Likewise, the African gardenia rarely succumbs to disease. However, it can fall victim to stem rot in overly moist conditions.

Certainly, the African gardenia doesn't knock your socks off with its enthusiasm, but it's a comely little plant. And it's so congenial. All you really need to successfully cultivate an African gardenia is patience. Several years might intervene before mitriostigma reaches a stature worth boasting about, but there are plenty of rewards while you wait.

Trachelospermums

In our home, interaction with our houseplants occurs primarily after working hours. We encounter our rex begonias by lamplight, and we rarely see the hibiscus with the sun shining through its petals. That's why there's a *Trachelospermum asiaticum* in the east window. When we trudge up the path at twilight after a long day's work and throw open the side door, a rush of perfume greets our return. It's a delicious scent reminiscent of honey heavily laced with cinnamon. The aroma might fill the house subtly during our lunch break, but it intensifies after dusk. Trachelospermum smells like home to us.

If you can't recall ever meeting *T. asiaticum* perhaps its kissing cousin, *T. jasminoides*, the pinwheel jasmine, will strike a familiar chord. Don't be thrown off by the common name. *Trachelospermum jasminoides* isn't a jasmine at all; it isn't even remotely related. The vine might *look* similar to jasmines because of its winding stems and dark-green, pointed leaves; it might *bloom* like a jasmine, with pearly white blossoms in small clusters; it might *smell* like a jasmine with a deep, intense perfume; but it isn't a jasmine.

So, if trachelospermum isn't a jasmine, what is it? Trachelospermums (formerly known by the equally unpronounceable name of rhynchospermum) are vining members of the family Apocynaceae, the same family to which allamandas and mandevillas belong. Native to China, *T. jasminoides*, the pinwheel jasmine, spends spring and summer smothered in a blizzard of inch-wide blossoms. Each flower has twisted petals, very much like a whirligig. It's a beautiful blossom, if you take a moment to study its structure close-up. And, in so doing, you might find yourself in just the right position to make some olfactory observations as well. From a distance, the pinwheel jasmine smells seductive. Nearby, it's incredibly heady.

Trachelospermum jasminoides is a vigorous vine with brittle, strong-willed stems that need a sizable trellis to support their excursions. You can count on devoting quite a chunk of window space to

The flowers of Trachelospermum asiaticum *are handsome enough, but their evening scent is absolutely intoxicating.*

this rampant wanderer. And you should also plan on spending a portion of your time weaving the vining branches into the support. Since the stems quickly become woody, discipline must be applied in the vine's formative stages.

Lesser known but more conducive to the confines of the average windowsill space, *T. asiaticum* is much smaller than the pinwheel jasmine and thus easier to handle indoors. The blossom clusters might not be as large, but the aroma is more intense and poignant. In my opinion, it's the trachelospermum to adopt into your windowsill.

The intricately winding stems have a sort of complexity that smacks of living sculpture. You can stare at those stems for a long time and never get bored. Our *T. asiaticum* is wound into a tight, two-foot-tall labyrinth composed of interwoven stems and small shiny leaves. Throughout spring, summer, and autumn, the plant is a maze not only of winding stems, but of clusters of small, five-petaled, wheat-colored blossoms as well. Visually, the flowers can't compete with the knock-'em-dead columneas or impatiens in the east window. And yet aromatically, *T. asiaticum* puts famed perfume plants such as jasmine to shame.

Both trachelospermums need assistance in training. But *T. asiaticum* can easily be woven into a compact mass of winding stems and deep green leaves, whereas *T. jasminoides* can't really be consolidated into anything smaller than a three-foot extravaganza. Besides the weaving chores, trachelospermums really don't demand much attention. Often enlisted as landscape plants in the Southwest, they rarely wilt. Even in summer, watering need not be done daily. And a trachelospermum would have to become mighty hungry before the shiny leaves turned from their luscious green to a paler hue. Fertilize the vine only in spring, summer, and early autumn once every four to six weeks with 20-20-20 or any balanced plant food.

Temperatures can range between 40 and 70 degrees Fahrenheit at night and 50 to 100 degrees during the day. Trachelospermums will endure the baking sun of a high-rise south window, the less intense rays of an east window, or the diffuse light of a west-facing sill. However, be sure to rotate this bulky vine regularly to expose all its angles to light. When blooming season arrives, you'll have a generous dappling of buds throughout.

Pruning a trachelospermum isn't really necessary. Instead, we just keep winding the vine around. The older branches might lose leaves, but that's OK—they provide a framework on which to intertwine the younger stems. In fact, the twiggy interior looks rather artistic—like a grapevine wreath. Grooming really isn't a frequent chore either. Spent leaves drop to the ground, and withered blossoms shrivel up and disappear.

Trachelospermums should be repotted in late winter just before the spring flush of new growth begins. Use a heavy soil with plenty of sand and compost. Since the roots don't drink ravenously, you can safely choose a clay container rather than plastic. Clay also provides an anchor for the heavy entanglement of stems aloft. Even with the clay ballast, our trachelospermum has taken occasional tumbles when the top-heavy crown is set askew by sill-sitting cats.

Scale and mealybugs are the only marauders to bother trachelospermums, and they're not frequent pests. In fact, few insects would even think of attacking such leathery leaves. In the plant world, a thick skin is the best defense.

After you've put in a long day at work, there's nothing more agreeable than an enthusiastic welcome home by a seductive fragrance. And what more can you ask than to sink into your favorite easy chair, prop up your feet, and rest your eyes upon a quietly beautiful botanical? If that plant requires very little care or feeding and virtually no upkeep, all the better.

Introduction

According to my husband's *Astronomical Calendar*, the east- and west-facing windows in our home should receive just about equal amounts of light in midsummer. However, from January through early spring, the balance is tipped toward the west—at that time of year, the sun lingers half an hour longer in the west before setting each day. In autumn, the advantage passes to east windows, when the sun tarries half an hour earlier in the morning compared to its tenure at eventide. But half an hour here or there doesn't make much difference from a plant's point of view. By and large, the light streaming through east and west windows should be roughly equal.

Somehow, though, it doesn't seem to work out that way in our home. Even at the height of summer, our unobstructed west windows don't receive as much light as their east-facing counterparts. I blame it on the weather pattern. For some reason, clouds tend to roll in by late afternoon, muting the influx of sunbeams.

From a gardener's standpoint, there are other subtle differences between east and west. First of all, since the sun doesn't work its way through west windows until day's end, the exposure tends to be cooler in homes such as ours with one central thermostat. And since houseplants should be watered in the morning, plants grown in a western exposure often have slightly moister soil for the bulk of the day unless you take great care to water frugally. But in most cases, the differences between east and west are minor, and a gardener might easily interchange the two exposures. You could take a fuchsia, a maranta, or a rex begonia and grow it in east or west windows, depending upon the design of your house and the flow of your family traffic.

Although every exposure of our house is well endowed with windows, our family doesn't seem to gravitate toward the west sector of our home. I blame it on the fact that we're basically morning people. We're rarely present to witness the sun's play through the west panes. In winter, the sun sets while we're still at work; in summer, everyone's

W
E
S
T

On the window ledge sits rex begonia 'Rainbow Warrior' not far from Calathea insignis; above hangs Hoya lacunosa *in flower.*

119

out in the garden by the time the sun has traveled to illuminate the west-facing rooms. Most of the heavily trafficked rooms overlook east or south. Yet there's one glaring exception. As you enter the front door, a west-facing window splashes light right into your path. A rex begonia sits proudly in the stream of its rays.

Alocasias

Generally, I am not a major fan of foliage plants. Like most folks, I'd just as soon have blossoms, if possible. And yet alocasias have a sophistication that makes flowers seem superfluous. Alocasias are architectural plants, building their image on clean, sleek lines. They are the epitome of simplicity, and yet they exude the soul of exotica. Few flowering plants make an equally succinct statement.

There's something rather masculine about these no-frills aroids, or members of the arum family (Araceae). Related to skunk cabbage and Jack-in-the-pulpits, alocasias bear insignificant and infrequent blossoms. Our alocasias have never shown the slightest desire to form flowers. But apparently we're not missing much—the blossoms are reputedly so pitiful that experienced gardeners suggest removing the buds before they sap vigor from those striking leaves.

The foliage really does capture your full attention. Leaf outlines range from heart-shaped to arrow-shaped, skeleton-cut, and every other foliar silhouette imaginable. The lines are sharp and dramatic, which seems appropriate for plants native to the heart of the jungle. But that's not all. Adding to the intrigue, alocasias often feature metallic coloration and contrasting veins. Unlike other foliage plants, alocasias never slip into the background—they dominate the scene.

A year ago, I brought *Alocasia watsoniana* home to study its intricate markings more closely, fully expecting to return it to the greenhouse the next morning. Familiarity bred affection and I couldn't part with it. The plant settled down happily in a west window. It hasn't

The plants in bedroom windows can be chosen to match the room's decor. Here a standard of Fuchsia 'Tom Thumb' *adorns a mantle, while below sit (left to right) rhizomatous begonia* B. crassicaulis, *rex begonia 'Fortune Cookie', and* Alocasia watsoniana.

Although it starts small, Alocasia watsoniana *can become quite sizable and boasts dramatic foliage.*

floored us with its progress, but it adds a nice accent to the decor. Every month, our alocasia sends up another gray, arrow-shaped leaf from the base. Gradually, the leaf stems grow longer until they tower three feet in the air, each foot-wide leaf accented by a raised gray midrib surrounded by a frantic confusion of squiggly gray lines. It's a piece of living art. And with very little care and only an occasional dusting, it always looks picture perfect.

Although *A. watsoniana* is the only alocasia that we've adopted into our home, several other species reside in the greenhouse. As I mentioned earlier, we're not strong on foliage plants. But who could resist the long, arrow-shaped, wavy-edged leaves of *A. sanderiana*, the Kris plant? Native to the Philippines, the lustrous, deep-green, shiny leaves eventually become nearly two feet in diameter, emblazoned with a zigzag of prominent, wide cream veins. The nearly identical *A. ×amazonica* assumes a slightly larger stance, sending its arrow-shaped leaves several feet into the air.

The Kris plant was our first alocasia, but it proved addictive and *A. cuprea* followed hastily on its heels. Native to Borneo and Malaysia, *A. cuprea* has broad, oval, nasturtiumlike leaves that look very much like exotic lily pads. Each leaf is deep rose with dark-green sunken veins etched in the surface, contrasting with a deep-maroon underside. Painfully slow-growing, *A. cuprea* is small by alocasia standards—the leaves never reach more than a foot in diameter, and the plant holds only a handful of leaves at a time. *Alocasia cuprea* says a lot in a few clean lines.

Most alocasias are one-sided affairs meant to be admired from a certain angle. In a window, they must be rotated continually if you want to see their best face. But *A. micholitziana* 'Green Velvet' turns its heart-shaped leaves in all directions. Horticulturists have been waging an ongoing battle concerning the lineage of 'Green Velvet': Some call it *A. maxkowskii* 'Green Velvet'; some say it's a hybrid of *A. sanderiana* or *A. amazonica*. I won't enter into the fray here—no matter what its origins happen to be, 'Green Velvet' is a gorgeous, easily grown alocasia with a generous crop of small, plush, satiny leaves etched with a cream midrib against a moss-green background.

Not only are alocasias a step above other foliage plants visually, they're also more challenging to cultivate. Most foliage plants are cast-iron affairs that endure all sorts of environmental insults with a stiff upper lip. Not so with alocasias. They are aristocrats among foliage plants, and they expect to be treated as such. Humidity levels must remain high (at least 50 percent) or their leaf tips shrivel. And a damaged leaf totally blights the fine-tuned effect. Overwatering and too much fertilizer will cause the same symptoms. Bright light results in immediate sunburning that blights the leaves, injures the stems, and virtually ruins your horticultural masterpiece in a few brief hours.

In their native habitats, alocasias often stretch their roots along limestone outcroppings. Given the plants' shallow, thick roots, many growers assume that alocasias prefer a peaty, soilless medium. However, I find that a good, stiff, heavy soil promotes fat stems that stand proudly upright and carry huge, nicely marked leaves at the tips. In a heavy soil, drinks must be served often or an alocasia wilts. On the other hand, you don't want to overwater—alocasias heartily detest soggy toes. Fertilize only once every four to six weeks. It's a delicate balance. You want to maintain good foliar color but discourage rank, gangly growth that will overwhelm your windowsill. Alocasias also show a marked preference for clay pots rather than plastic. Certainly, when architecture is the theme, clay seems the most sympathetic element.

Alocasias demand warm temperatures: The thermometer shouldn't slip much lower than 65 degrees Fahrenheit at night. Cold alocasias will blanch and show poor contrast in the leaves. As long as the humidity remains high, the temperature can soar during the day. Sprinkling the leaves with water keeps the shiny surfaces lustrous and adds to the moisture in the air.

With alocasias, your only mission is maintaining the perfection of that handsome foliage. Fortunately, you don't have to battle bugs in your campaign. Insects wouldn't even dream of chewing on those thick, metallic leaves. With alocasias, all of nature conspires to clad the window exotically with a minimum of fuss and bother.

Anthuriums

Anthuriums are living proof that weird and wonderful things can happen on a west window. At first glance, anthuriums masquerade as foliage plants with comely, slender leaves. But that's just the beginning: Most anthuriums feature flowers as well, and those blossoms are some of the windowsill's most startling inflorescences.

If current fashions in yard ornaments hold any sway indoors, then I figure that flamingo flowers—the common name of several anthuriums—should be making a strong showing on the windowsill right about now. After all, they're bedecked in colors that trendy gardeners crave. Amid a glade of slender, pale-green and rose-tinged leaves, the bizarre blossoms jut akimbo. As with all members of the arum family (Araceae) the gaudy spadix-and-cloak affair for which anthuriums are famous is technically an inflorescence—it's not actually a single flower, but rather a multitude of many minute flowers lining the spadix. Whatever you call them, the blossoms look decidedly unreal, like the sort of flower that Lewis Carroll might have dreamt up—all waxy and graphically veined with a strange, noselike protuberance poking from the center. The form is notable, but it's the quirky color combinations that really catch your eye.

The most commonly grown flamingo flower is *Anthurium scherzerianum*, which sports a folded back, shocking-pink cloak that contrasts with the curly bright-orange spadix. Despite the kinky colors, *A. scherzerianum* has quite a bit of snob appeal—flamingo flowers are expensive little entities to obtain. Fortunately, you don't need to invest much time or bother in *A. scherzerianum*'s upkeep—those absurd blossoms are easily entertained in the average home. The cultivar 'Rothschildianum' is equally appropriate for anyone's west-facing sill, but it's not as easy to find on the market. It takes the absurdity of the plain species one step further with random red speckles on its large, white, textured cloak—like bloodstains on creased linen—and then tops off the show by balancing a long, curly spadix above.

Another species known as the flamingo flower (much to everyone's confusion), the South American *A. andraeanum* fetches a high price and is not entirely comfortable in the average home. Humidity levels are rarely sufficient to keep this denizen of the jungle thriving. And yet if you've got the moisture, *A. andraeanum* is the flamingo flower to cultivate—its blossoms are big, glossy, and decidedly artnouveauish, with a lipstick-red, heart-shaped, intricately veined cloak surrounding a long, straight, lemon-yellow spadix. Stranger still, there's a pure white version of *A. andraeanum* called 'Album' with a spotless white cloak behind its rigid orange spadix. Additional hybrids feature equally odd and otherworldly color combinations that stretch the imagination and invariably cause passersby to stop and take a second look.

Not all anthuriums boast ravishing blossoms. Several species are grown solely for their ornamental foliage. We've underplanted some of our greenhouse beds with *A. clarinervium*, a species from southern Mexico. Most visitors mistake it for a philodendron when they first encounter its foot-long, heart-shaped, olive-green leaves enhanced by striking cream veins. But this foliage plant is far more finicky than any philodendron you're likely to meet. Atmospheric moisture is es-

One of the most gaudily clad flowers available for a west window, Anthurium scherzerianum 'Rothschildianum' *sends out a generous supply of exotic blooms.*

sential to *A. clarinervium*'s health and welfare, and in the greenhouse, it receives plenty. Such high humidity levels might prove difficult to achieve in the average home, unless you can house your anthurium in a west-facing bathroom window—with the shades left immodestly undrawn, of course. Misting does the waxy leaves no harm, and a periodic spritzing keeps the foliage sparkling and momentarily raises the atmospheric moisture.

As far as the flowering varieties are concerned, anyone can keep an anthurium reasonably happy and healthy, but it takes a little expertise to grow a fantastic, blossom-studded specimen. Light is no problem—a bright west or east window will suffice. But don't attempt to increase blossoms by cranking up the footcandles: In a southern exposure, anthuriums sunburn hideously or bleach to a sickly pale shade. The secrets to robust anthuriums lie not in light, but in growing methods.

Frequent division is the most important factor in promoting flowers. A Hawaiian friend passed along the tip—if you want your anthurium to burst into blossom, remove all the pups. At first I was skeptical. After all, anthuriums look so much better as dense clumps of small foliage rather than solitary offsets with a few tall, lonely leaves. But, of course, flowers are the soul of an anthurium; the foliage acts merely as a foil. So I divided up an older plant that had stubbornly refused to blossom for several years. Within a few months, the divisions were cheerfully blossoming their hearts out and the flowers were twice the size of their undivided counterparts. Now I'm convinced—anthuriums do not like crowding.

Dividing isn't the easiest job in the world. Anthurium roots are thick, brittle, and fond of intertwining. Wrestling them apart requires a combination of muscle, dexterity, and unfailing patience. When you do manage to untangle the roots of each crown, repot the divisions individually into wide, shallow containers—an anthurium's expansive root system likes to stretch out.

When repotting or dividing, be sure to use long-fibered sphagnum moss rather than soil. Anthuriums prefer a fluffy substrate as long as they're fertilized more frequently (once every two to three weeks with 20-20-20) to compensate for the lean medium. My Hawaiian friend also advised setting the crown a little above the surrounding soil so the anthurium looks as if it's preparing to erupt out of its pot. The resulting plant might seem desperately in need of tamping down, but the anthurium invariably rewards us with flowers. And when an anthurium makes blossoms, the show is not only spectacular, it's also a lengthy affair: Those waxy inflorescences last in pristine form for several months. In the meantime, you're home free. No insects disrupt the show; no fuss or bother is required to maintain the display. Your only chore will be convincing visitors that those shiny, almost plastic-looking blossoms are real.

Camellias

Winter is a camellia's season to shine. Just as surely as spring is associated with forced tulips and hyacinths, midwinter is camellia time indoors. And it's a good plant for a difficult juncture. If ever there was a blossom designed to play counterpoint against winter's bleakness, it is the soft, pastel-hued camellia. Even stubbornly practical, severely unpoetic, and congenitally nonromantic souls fall under its spell.

Camellias have been taking the sting out of winter for quite some time. Yet when the first camellias arrived on European shores in the 1730s, they were greeted with something less than unabashed joy. As the story goes, the East India Company was eagerly expecting a shipment of tea (*Camellia sinensis*) when they received cartons filled with the closely related but unbeverage-worthy *C. japonica* instead. For tea drinkers, it was a most unpleasant switch. For ornamental horticulture, it was a fortunate moment.

Eventually, everyone embraced *C. japonica* with open arms. When most people think of camellias, they usually conjure up a vision of *C. japonica* with its treelike linear branches dappled by immense, fluffy-petaled blossoms. In their native Japan, japonicas are called *tsubaki*, the tree with shining leaves. Even during the summer when camellias haven't a flower to be seen, they still make handsome houseplants thanks to that dense, deep-green, polished foliage. But as soon as buds start to swell in December, the foliage is completely forgotten. Instead, attention focuses on those huge, four- to six-inch, unfolding flowers. Some look like single or double roses; others mimic peonies or anemones with uncanny accuracy. And camellias are impeccably color coordinated. A collection displayed together makes a harmonious medley in various shades of white, pink, plush red, and yellow, with petals frequently enhanced by speckling, splashing, streaking, or picotee edges.

Camellia japonica may be the superstar, but *C. sasanqua* deserves

A radiator no longer in use provides a stand for the rex begonia 'Curly Fireflush' with Camellia sasanqua *'Chansonette' (left) and the rhizomatous begonia 'Silver Jewel' below.*

Camellia japonica 'Bob Hope' has frilly, early-season flowers with just a hint of fragrance, each boasting a nest of pollen-laden stamens.

wider acclaim. Sasanquas have much smaller, daintier blossoms than the japonicas, but the overall picture is equally impressive. Buds adorn sasanqua stems with all the poetry and profusion of appleblossoms. And sasanqua flowers often feature the bonus of a subtle yet sweet scent. Even the shape of a sasanqua is reminiscent of something you might find in an orchard, for sasanquas spread their branches horizontally to form a shapely silhouette. Sasanquas begin blooming earlier in the season than japonicas—usually in October—and the flowers can continue for months under cool conditions. But topmost on the sasanquas' list of virtues is the fact that sasanquas are slightly easier than japonicas to coax into flower.

While anyone can grow a camellia, not everyone can make it bloom. Beneath a camellia's frilly exterior lurks a plant that stubbornly refuses to perform unless it's given a winter-long dose of frigid air. In practical terms, this means temperatures below 50 degrees Fahrenheit at night—colder if possible. The sun can warm the bush during the day and the thermometer can rise sky-high during the summer. But when the heating season arrives, these Japanese natives drop their buds dramatically the moment they receive a shot of forced hot air. And a big, plump, promising bud lying at your feet is quite possibly the plant world's most heart-wrenching sight.

Although japonicas are unwavering in their desire for unmitigated cold, sasanquas will settle for a mildly uncomfortable 55 degrees when buds are first setting; after that crucial period, they can take even warmer temperatures. Still, few homeowners want to endure the Big Chill for the sake of a few fantastic flowers. In modern homes, camellias are usually confined to sun porches or unheated entryways.

Matters of temperature aside, camellias are a cinch. They bask in the indirect rays of a west-facing window, and they don't demand high humidity or frequent watering, although the drinks should be increased slightly in late summer and autumn to set buds. At other times of year, you can safely let a camellia go slightly thirsty. Fertilizing should also be accomplished primarily in summer and early autumn, with applications of 20-20-20 every four weeks. An occasional brisk bath keeps scale—the only bug to bother camellias—at bay. Camellias respond well to frequent repotting in a very heavy, very humusy, and slightly acid soil (a pH of 6.0 is optimal). Even under the most favorable conditions, camellias are slow-growing shrubs, making about a foot of headway annually. With age, the progress slows to about three inches of new growth per year. Thus pruning needn't be a frequent undertaking, although some tip-pinching early in a camellia's career will encourage branching toward the base.

Because we've never attempted to heat the entire expanse of our rambling Victorian home, the west window of an unheated library provides the perfect nook for a camellia. It doesn't receive many casual visitors in winter. In fact, for a few months, the only news we hear of the plant is when some brave volunteer makes a quick dash with the watering pot and comes back to report (with chattering teeth) that all is well. The moment buds begin to swell and show color, the plant is proudly trundled into the heart of the home where its performance can be enjoyed without donning coat and gloves. Since the entire house is rather drafty, the buds don't blast and flowers hold on for a month or more. We're mighty grateful for the show.

Actually, we feel privileged. Camellias are our reward for living a stoic life-style and saving on the fuel bill. People make pilgrimages to see those fluffy-petaled blossoms. And if the crop is bountiful and the visitors are friends, we send them home with a few flowers to float in a shallow dish of water. If you can't grow a camellia, at least cultivate a close relationship with someone who can.

Cissus

My first encounter with cissus came minutes after arriving at college for my freshman year. Having just dragged some severely overstuffed trunks up the dormitory stairs, I opened the door of the cubby that was to be my home for the next semester and found my new roommate carefully twining a *Cissus rhombifolia* around the windowsill. It was a grape ivy, she explained, and we had inherited it.

As it turned out, my roommate and I were grossly mismatched. That introductory conversation was one of our few civil exchanges. While she took ballet, I enrolled in a composting course. She sprayed the room with cheap perfume, while I tracked mud on the carpet. We spent the entire semester trying to be rid of each other. We were never granted a switch, but if we had succeeded in changing rooms, there would've been a very nasty squabble for custody of the cissus.

Few plants can tolerate a college dorm, but the grape ivy was perfectly content to wander around the window frame in that dry, overheated, stuffy, poorly lit room. Ever since, I've harbored a warm affection for *C. rhombifolia*. True, grape ivy isn't the most exciting vine in the world to have hanging about. But if you find sheer energy and dogged fortitude fascinating, a grape ivy is the vine to adopt.

When I look at *C. rhombifolia*, poison ivy comes to mind more readily than grape vines. The shiny, trifoliate leaves and vining stems can give you pause at first glance. Of course, gardeners have nothing to fear from cissus as far as skin irritation is concerned. But still, a word of caution is in order: Grape ivy is just as grabby and fast-paced as anything else that has earned the nickname of ivy. If you need to cover ground (or anything else, for that matter), cissus is ideal.

Cissus are primarily foliage plants. Only *C. adenopoda* forms a lacework of dainty blossoms worth mentioning. The most popular cissus are the grape ivy, mentioned above (*C. rhombifolia*) and its larger-leaved counterpart, *C. r.* 'Ellen Danica'. Although it's not readily available at every nursery, *C. r.* 'Mandaiana' is the cultivar I prefer to keep around as a reminder of college days. The leaves are only one-third the size of the species and they form dense mounds like mosaics of sharply cut foliage. Compared to its standard-size relatives, 'Mandaiana' is rather endearing and certainly easier to keep within bounds. Tinier still is *C. striata*, a species from South America with lacy, skeleton-cut, trifoliate leaves. The thumbnail-size foliage clusters densely along the vining stems, making it a perfect volunteer for covering topiary hoops, but progress is slow because of its minute dimensions.

Ten years ago, the kangaroo vine (*C. antarctica*)—native to Australia, naturally—could be found in supermarkets far and wide. But the public soon tired of that indefatigable vine with its unremarkable, leathery, oval leaves. Try though you might, it's impossible to kill a kangaroo vine, and I suspect that people grew weary of trying politely to do it in. Undoubtedly they also became irked when that stubborn vine patently refused to be pruned into shape. No matter how sternly you snip the rigid tips of a kangaroo vine, it never agrees to go where you want or fork when you want—it just stubbornly ambles along a straight and narrow path with few branches and fewer frills. In my opinion, life is too short and windowsill space is too precious to waste on kangaroo vines.

Cissus adenopoda is far more thrilling. Native to tropical West Africa, this plush vine is covered with soft pink velveteen that begs to be petted—just like the famed purple passion plant (*Gynura sarmentosa*). In addition to fuzz, the plant also sports lacy umbels of elderlike flowers that stretch out amid the frill of wheat-colored, curly tendrils. Although all cissus are acrobatic, *C. adenopoda* is invariably a far-flung affair compared to its dense, tightly knit kin, thanks to the lengthy grasp of its aggressive tendrils. Although the vine will survive in a west window, an unobstructed eastern or southern expo-

sure enhances the color and density of the foliar fur while the distance between leaves is shortened under the influence of additional sun.

Although most cissus cheerfully tolerate hot air or cold, drought as well as drowning, *C. adenopoda* does not share the familial ability to endure abuse. The soft growing tips can be killed if the environment is too hot or cold. During the day 70 to 80 degrees Fahrenheit is preferable, while at night the thermometer shouldn't sink much lower than 55 degrees. Water the vine when the soil is dry to the touch. When in doubt, it's best to err on the side of thirstiness. *Cissus adenopoda* doesn't wilt easily but it resents excessive moisture underfoot. Rather than trying to convince *C. adenopoda* to branch, wind the flexible stems back around themselves to give the impression of fullness.

Cissus discolor doesn't really belong in this chapter, but it is too beautiful to ignore. Although it is undeniably a cissus, it hardly looks or acts like other members of the family. To begin with, the rex begonia vine, as it's often called, would definitely pout in a west-facing window. This Southeast Asian native needs bright southerly light to promote good foliar color. And that color is worth nurturing. Thanks to its gloriously patterned foliage, *C. discolor* far outshines any other cissus in cultivation. Confusing as it may be, the nickname "rex begonia vine" aptly describes *C. discolor*'s intricately marked foliage. Each broad, deeply textured four-to-six-inch leaf is handsomely striped purple, cream, and green, with a deep-maroon underside. In spring, when light levels increase, the foliar colors gain definition, making them especially radiant beside the duller winter growth. Meanwhile, the stems and tendrils are dark red, although the stems are hidden beneath the layers of overlapping arrow-shaped leaves. *Cissus discolor* is definitely a head-turning vine, especially considering its heft: In half a year, with a little initial pruning to encourage branching toward the base and some strategic twining of the tips, the rex begonia vine will grow at least three feet in diameter.

Like *C. adenopoda*, the rex begonia vine is also intolerant of overwatering, underwatering, and chilly temperatures. At night, it shouldn't be subjected to temperatures lower than 65 degrees. In the summer, when temperatures climb, *C. discolor* will flag, especially if

—

Cissus discolor is the exception to the rule for the genus—it needs a bright location to maintain good leaf color.

—

135

the foliage is close to the windowpanes. Move it out of the strong midday rays, give the leaves a light misting, and the vine will be as good as new. But don't try the misting trick in winter—the tissue-thin leaves are prone to fungal infections. Instead, keep the atmospheric moisture elevated by means of a humidifier or pebble tray.

Although other cissus are rarely visited by insects thanks to their leather-thick leaves, *C. discolor* can be plagued by slugs. However, when checking *C. discolor* for pests, don't panic when you discover clear, round, egglike masses on the undersides of the leaves and occasionally on the stems. The tiny round orbs of gel might look disconcerting, but they're actually harmless exudations naturally produced by the foliage.

There are other cissus in cultivation. In fact, there's a whole contingent of vining, sparsely foliated, swollen-stemmed cissus that are usually classified as succulents. Most of the succulent cissus demand bright light, sandy soil, and very little water to thrive. There are also rhoicissus and parthenocissus that are equally tolerant of less-than-perfect growing conditions but are generally too rambunctious to be accommodated in the average window. And really, it would be hard to improve on the easily grown, easily obtained, always amiable grape ivy as a roommate.

Fuchsias

Fuchsias are a summertime affair. Just when the garden outdoors demands our full attention, that's when fuchsias kick in. At the very beginning of summer, baskets overflowing with puffy fuchsia flowers are peddled high and low for Mother's Day. By the time Memorial Day rolls around, those very same baskets can be found dangling proudly from the eaves of front porches up and down Main Street. They might be laden with a heavy crop of eye-riveting flowers for a month or two, but outdoor-grown fuchsias always begin to look a little washed-out and stressed when the Fourth of July parade marches past. Just between you and me, fuchsias are more comfortable left indoors on a cool, comfortable, west-facing windowsill.

Fuchsias come in all shapes and sizes to please a variety of tastes. On one hand you have those chubby Mother's Day types with broad leaves, a robust habit, a heft reaching two to three feet in diameter, and a thick dressing of tutu-like double flowers. They come in an array of incredible colors: royal-purple sepals above a screaming-magenta corolla; pale-pink petals above a deep-blush corolla; snow-white sepals with radiant-cherry corolla; and so on—and of course the reverse of each combination can be found as well. In case that weren't enough, matching pistil and stamens jut from the corolla's flared skirts. The doubles are the showstoppers of the family, designed to knock the socks off your mother and anyone else who might happen to catch a glimpse.

Single fuchsias aren't nearly as popular with the Mother's Day crowd, but I prefer their subtle charms. And I bet your mom would agree. When contemplating the single fuchsia, it's easy to see why the flowers were originally called lady's eardrops. They call to mind bright, sleek, dangly jewelry. Although singles sport the same profusion of unabashed colors as their double counterparts, the dimensions are smaller—they reach only about two feet in width—so the whole shebang seems toned down. Each blossom might be simpler, but the quantity is increased. Singles spend summer smothered in bloom.

Actually, it's the dwarf single fuchsias that really tug at my heartstrings. There's something endearing about the dwarfs. The flowers are only an inch long at most, but each is a tiny work of art, and hundreds of them line the thin stems. The leaves that clothe the squat (two feet wide) but broad (one foot tall) plants are about the size of your smallest fingernail. I should think that anyone would fall head over heels for 'Papoose', 'Bluette', 'Buttons & Bows', or 'Tom Thumb'.

Whether the fuchsia you choose is large or small, they all prefer the same growing conditions. Most folks fail with fuchsias the moment they plunk them in a sunny spot. When fuchsias are faced with unfiltered sun, they will wilt within an hour, and if the transgression is not remedied with haste, your fuchsia will scorch beyond recovery. Even in a west-facing window it would be wise to partially draw the curtain during blazing summer afternoons. Similarly, if you must put your fuchsia on the porch, check the location carefully for stray sunrays throughout the day before hanging the plant out.

Sun is not the only reason fuchsias wilt. They're also quick to fizzle for lack of water during hot, dry weather. And once the foliage droops, it won't perk up again for an hour or two after watering. It

Pleasingly subtle in its flower shades, Fuchsia *'Madame Dachau' is extremely prolific and easy to please; in front is* Bougainvillea *'Double Red'.*

also helps to dampen the leaves while serving drinks during spring and summer. But don't try that trick in fall and winter. Fuchsias rest during the winter months, so keep both foliage and roots dry at that time. By the same token, encourage vigorous spring and summer growth with frequent feeding (once every three to four weeks), but withhold fertilizer in winter. And repot only in the flush of new spring growth, using a fluffy but rich soil. Fuchsias prefer plenty of space to stretch out their roots, so give them a squat but broad pot.

Although dwarf fuchsias tend to be self-branching, other types need pinching to encourage side shoots. After an initial spring shearing, fuchsias take the initiative themselves and expand rapidly. Of course, hybridizers have lent a helping hand by providing plants that assume just the form you desire without constant coaching. If the bloomer is destined to dangle from your front porch, select a fuchsia bred as a hanging plant. (I favor 'Cascade' or 'Pink Cloud'.) On the other hand, if you fancy an upright affair, try 'Cherrie Pie' (a noteworthy new hybrid with striking blue and red single flowers) or 'Voodoo' among the regular-size hybrids.

Fuchsias are famous for the ease with which they can be coaxed into standard or tree form. Simply encourage the main stem straight upward for two or three feet and then pinch it out to expand into a crown of showering blossoms. If you start in late winter, you can craft a finished standard by summer's end. But, to avoid heartache, be sure to give a standard a sturdy support, especially if it's bound for the porch—the stems are brittle and break easily in a strong breeze. The Victorians honed fuchsia training into a fine art and were fond of fitting the plants with umbrella supports. The fuchsias apparently responded well to this treatment, developing into canopies so broad that a twosome could easily hide underneath. If that's your goal, any upright hybrid is appropriate, but my personal favorite for standardizing is 'Hidcote Beauty', which boasts a graceful habit along with a tendency to blossom throughout the hottest summer months with a bountiful crop of dainty coral and white blossoms.

Most fuchsias go into a slump when fall rolls around, and by the time winter arrives, all is over. The only fuchsias to blossom doggedly throughout the winter are the pink-flowering, mahogany-leaved 'Honeysuckle' and its parent 'Gartenmeister Bonstedt', an heirloom variety introduced in 1905. Other fuchsias slowly peter out until there isn't a blossom left. Don't panic if they drop leaves as well. Keep them dry but not parched.

Some gardeners let fuchsias go totally dormant in winter, pulling them away from the light. We take the opposite approach and push them closer to the windowpanes. Increased light doesn't prompt fuchsias to perform great feats of bravery during the winter, but it ensures a less spindly, stronger base when growth resumes in spring. During the winter, fuchsias can withstand quite cool temperatures (ours are regularly subjected to 40 degree nights) as long as you keep the foliage dry. In spring, at the first hint of new growth, give your fuchsia a stern clipping to rid it of floppy winter growth and to encourage vigorous basal branching.

During summer heatwaves, porch- and garden-grown fuchsias also slip into a lull. To encourage flowers when temperatures sizzle, keep the foliage misted and the plants in a breezy location.

Fuchsias aren't carefree plants. They're prone to red spider mites, whiteflies, and aphids. Keep your eyes peeled for all these foes. A strong and frequent jetstream of chilly water deters pests while also perking up flagging foliage.

Grooming is an important issue for fuchsias. Lower leaves that turn yellow and yet still hang stubbornly on should be removed. At the same time, clip off the spent flowers before they swell into fruit. The fruit is ornamental, but it steals energy that would otherwise be cycled into blossom production.

Hoyas

If you didn't inherit a hoya from your grandmother or great-aunt, chances are that you know someone who did. Apparently, at one time, everyone had a hoya hanging about, and those tenacious plants have a longevity that far surpasses the human life-span.

The hoya most often inherited is *Hoya carnosa*, known as the wax plant for its thick, succulent, waxy-surfaced leaves. First introduced in 1802 from its native China, Burma, and India, *H. carnosa* had plenty of time to gather thunder before your grandmother began her gardening career. By the end of the nineteenth century, wax plants were as omnipresent as aspidistras in the caverns of the average parlor.

Hoya carnosa is endowed with the sort of personality that fits the parlor perfectly. It can endure low humidity, low light levels, and drastic fluctuations in temperature, all of which make it equally suitable for the average city apartment. But *H. carnosa* only blossoms at a ripe old age. Chances are that your grandmother waited patiently for several years before she saw a single bud. In the meantime, the vine sent ropelike chains of leathery leaves roving about, while your

Hoya serpens *is grown primarily for its tiny foliage; the flowers are insignificant.*

grandmother carefully tucked them around the window frame. Simultaneously, thick roots roamed underground, filling their container to the point of bursting. But back then, people didn't repot frequently. And anyway, repotting a vine with appendages reaching halfway around the room was not an easy feat. Eventually, blossoms began to appear here and there along the stem and continued to form regularly thereafter.

That is, the hoya bloomed faithfully until the next generation took over. Filled with determination to do right by an ancestral plant, a flurry of repotting and feeding always seems to follow acquisition of a family heirloom. Of course, the plant doesn't complain. Unless hoyas are seriously abused, they just go on about their slow existence. But they don't reward your fussing with a crop of flowers. And the blossoms are such a plus. All hoya flowers feature different configurations on a common star-within-a-star theme. *Hoya carnosa* has a creamy-white five-pointed star with a smaller, similarly colored star within accented by an even tinier red frill in the center. Each flower is only one-half inch wide, but the blossoms are massed in plump clusters of a dozen or more held close to the deep-green, waxy leaves. The flowers make all those months of concentrated neglect seem worth the effort.

Although *H. carnosa* may have been the choice of the Victorians, it's not the only hoya on the horizon now. Far from it. With over two hundred species and an incredible diversity of leaf shapes and sizes available as well as a multitude of varying star-within-a-star combinations to select from, collectors can have a field day. Fortunately, most hoyas exhibit the same iron-cast fortitude that first won the hearts of indoor gardeners generations ago.

Being an impatient person, I prefer hoyas that blossom willingly without a wait. And nowadays, there are plenty of species that oblige. You can also select a favorite scent. Hoya blossoms emit an incredible repertoire of aromas ranging from hot mocha to warm cinnamon. In many cases, the perfume intensifies after dark—a trait that is always popular with gardeners who see their plants only at the end of the workday.

Since there are so many hoyas around, I'll confine myself to describing a handful of easy-blooming personal favorites. *Hoya pubera*, a species from Java introduced in 1826, definitely tops the list. The leaves are oval, only one to two inches long, and they huddle closely along tight vines. But the main attraction is definitely the winter-

Throughout the winter, just when you need flowers the most, Hoya pubera *is speckled with star-shaped umbels that emit an aroma of hot mocha.*

blooming flower clusters that stud the stem profusely. Composed of ten to twelve tiny star-shaped flowers, they emit a distinct essence of hot chocolate that gets stronger after dark. Despite its country of origin, *H. pubera* tolerates low humidity and considerable abuse from gardeners who might forget to water now and then. It's only failing is that *H. pubera* is painfully slow-growing.

Smaller still is *H. lacunosa* from Thailand and Malaysia, with long, thin leaves on meandering, limp stems. I wouldn't really rank this species as one of the world's most ravishing hoyas. In fact, the umbels are so small and inconspicuous that they might easily be overlooked until the moment they send a heady hint of cinnamon floating through the room. By evening, the scent intensifies into something quite seductive. Although most hoyas tolerate coolness, the tiny leaves of *H. lacunosa* shrivel when nighttime temperatures dip below 60 degrees Fahrenheit.

Most hoyas send ropes of foliage wandering about and thus look like rather uncontrollable affairs. However, *H. lanceolata* subsp. *bella* (formerly *H. l. bella*) goes against the prevailing image. This subspecies from Himalaya and Burma drapes its container with neat sets of elliptic leaves. But there's more to *H. l.* subsp. *bella* than merely handsome foliage. Through most of the year, a constellation of small, fragrant flowers nods from the undersides of the leaf sets.

Compared to most hoyas, *H. lanceolata* subsp. *bella* is a finicky little animal. Without abundant humidity, the tiny leaves shrivel. If you forget to water once too often, the same thing happens. Strong sun has a similar effect, and temperatures below 55 degrees can produce equally devastating results. Fortunately, the plant usually snaps out of its slump after a rather long pouting period, so don't give up hope. To prevent the whole scenario, monitor the leaves constantly for signs of wrinkling. At the same time, watch for blanching from leprechaun green to a paler hue. At the first signs of stress, take immediate steps to remedy the situation.

Of the larger, more rambunctious hoyas, I favor the Japanese native *H. motoskei* with its large, rounded leaves and equally prominent umbels dripping with sweet nectar. In this case, each flower's soft outer star is palest pink, while the raised inner corona is sparkling maroon. Individual flowers are one-half inch wide and the umbel holds more than a dozen blossoms that remain in prime condition for months, all the while exuding the mouthwatering aroma of piping-hot croissants. Not only is *H. motoskei* handsome, it comes a close second to *H. carnosa* as far as ease of cultivation is concerned. Your primary responsibility will be to marshall the brittle stems into some semblance of shape. If left to their own devices, they flail haphazardly into outer space.

Equally energetic if not more so is *H. purpureofusca*, a species from Indonesia with long, slender, mottled leaves on thin vines. Striking foliage is a feature of this species. In a well-lit western window, the silver speckles gain color, blushing pink. The flowers are large, long-lasting, and plentifully packed in dense clusters of fuzzy, deep-pink stars that emit a delightful scent. *Hoya purpureofusca* grows just as rampantly as *H. motoskei*, but its whiplike stems are much more pliable and easier to coax into shape. And the blushing leaves endure higher light levels than most hoyas, although the vine is perfectly content to wind around a west-facing window.

Not all hoyas are grown for their flowers. In some cases, the foliage predominates and flowers are superfluous. *Hoya obovata*, the heart-leaved hoya, is a case in point. Who needs blossoms when all eyes are fixed upon the aerial display of huge, thick, rigid, three- to four-inch-wide heart-shaped leaves? Although *H. obovata* is not a fast grower, its rope-thick stems stubbornly jut at odd angles, which makes the heart-leaved display all the more fascinating but can prove a problem when you're trying to impose discipline. The only solution is to forcibly bend the stems when they're young and supple.

Another hoya grown for foliage is *H. compacta*, the so-called Hindu rope plant, with folded, crinkly leaves that line the stem so densely that the vine seems to cascade in a series of sailor's knots. Supposedly it does flower, although I've never witnessed the feat, and the blossoms are reputedly almond-scented. But here again, blossoms are not the main attraction.

Throughout the generations, hoyas have earned a reputation as no-fuss houseplants. And with few exceptions, that's true. One word of caution: Although some denizens of the west sill wouldn't mind receiving a little more light from an east or even a south window, hoyas are not among them. They blanch, shrivel, and scorch when sunrays fall directly on the foliage.

Hoyas tend to hail from humid regions of the world and they might appreciate a moist environment in your home. But it's certainly not necessary—they grow perfectly happily in a dry atmosphere. All hoyas prefer a cramped container to an oversize pot. A heavy, sandy, cactus-type soil works best underfoot. When choosing a container, clay is definitely preferable. Not only does clay drain more readily, it also provides the ballast necessary to keep the weighty vines from toppling. Most hoyas either cascade limply downward (*H. compacta, H. lacunosa,* and *H. lanceolata* subsp. *bella*) or send their vines upwards winding around a trellis (*H. carnosa, H. motoskei, H. obovata,* and *H. purpureofusca*). When choosing a trellis, select something sturdy that you might want to live with for a long time—it's nearly impossible to unwind the ropelike stems once they've begun their ascent.

Hoyas prefer moderate feeding—fertilize once a month while they're in active growth. Water should also be applied sparingly, but never let the foliage wrinkle. After that, you're home free. Besides an occasional stray mealybug, pests don't bother the thick, succulent foliage. Actually, hoyas are the perfect plants for a gardener's weekend home. They perform over a long period and wait patiently for a little care.

Marantas and Calatheas

In every plant family, there's always one easy-growing relative. The rest of the family members might be impossibly finicky, but you can always find one species willing to settle down happily as a houseplant. In the family Marantaceae, that mercifully complaisant member is *Maranta leuconeura* var. *kerchoveana*, otherwise known as the rabbit's track plant for the prominent brown markings on its rounded leaves. You'll see its brown-spotted leaves lounging in restaurants and bank lobbies quietly collecting dust but still thriving. You've probably received a rabbit's track maranta for the grand opening of your new office or the birth of your new baby. People send them as gifts when they know that the recipient needs a little greenery in his or her life but won't have much time for coddling plants. The rabbit's track isn't the most exciting plant in the world, but it does the job.

Actually, there's much more to the Marantaceae than the rabbit's track plant. If you're willing to fuss a little over your houseplants, there are plenty of ravishing marantas and calatheas to grow in a humid west-facing window. You'll catch me continually mentioning marantas and calatheas in the same breath—the two genera are botanical Bobsey Twins. And really, only experts can tell the difference. Apparently, the flowers of calatheas are in racemes whereas they come in clusters on marantas. But flowers are an afterthought for most marantas and calatheas. Blossoms are an infrequent occurrence, and when they do pop up they're scarcely worth noticing. The real show is the foliage.

Of the thirty-two maranta species in cultivation, only a handful have entered the limelight. One of my personal favorites is *M. bicolor*, a species from South America with long, shiny, oval leaves marked with feather patterns in varying shades of green. The foliage is large— three to four inches long—and, during the day, each leaf lays flat against its neighbors. The result is a Sherwood Forest–like lushness. At night, the foliage folds upward like clasped hands, which explains why all marantas are commonly called prayer plants.

Bathroom windows take advantage of abundant humidity. In this well-lit west-facing window sit rhizomatous begonia 'Lime Swirl' (left) and Calathea zebrina *(right).*

Even though *M. bicolor* has caught my eye, the rest of the world scarcely knows that it exists. Apparently, they're preoccupied with *M. leuconeura* and its varieties. I've already given *M. leuconeura* var. *kerchoveana* its due. Far more intriguing, however, is *M. leuconeura* 'Massangeana', with burgundy and forest-green leaves marked with silver. Still more exotic is *M. leuconeura* var. *erythroneura*, which adds bright red streaks to the whole shebang.

These enhanced *M. leuconeura* varieties are almost as easy to cultivate as the plain old rabbit's track. Almost, but not quite. Only *M. l. kerchoveana* can survive lengthy periods of neglect. Its close cousins prefer—and deserve—better treatment. Give them even moisture underfoot and at least 30 to 40 percent humidity. And set them close to the panes on your west-facing windowsill—good light highlights their luscious foliar colors.

Compared to the meager list of marantas, the roster of calatheas in cultivation is quite impressive. No fewer than three hundred calathea species have been brought back from the jungles of tropical America. Of that number, a whopping twenty or more are readily available. Each calathea features its own unique combination of streaks, feathers, bars, spots, speckles, and stripes. I'm partial to several species, including *Calathea musaica*, with a haphazard web of dark-green, pencil-thin lines against a yellow background; *C. zebrina*, with tall, soft, satiny leaves zebra-striped in deep-olive green; *C. makoyana*, with luminous green-and-rose peacock feathering against a cream background; *C. rosea-picta*, with pink etchings enhancing the midrib and a dwarf growth habit; and *C. lancifolia* (formerly *C. insignis*), with slender, shiny, wavy leaves patterned with forest green on the upperside and backed by glistening maroon. Calatheas are all handsome, they all look ravishing side by side, and they're all rather difficult to grow. The problem lies in the fact that these deep jungle plants need both warm 65-degree-and-up temperatures and high humidity—nothing less than 50 percent will suffice and 60 percent is preferable. If you can indulge that little whim with a humidifier, you've got more than half the battle licked.

In their native habitats, marantas and calatheas dwell in the well-drained but fluffy jungle soil shaded by a diffuse canopy of foliage

—

This handsomely streaked version of Maranta arundinacea *is one of the easier members of the genus to grow.*

overhead. To translate that into your living room, members of the Marantaceae prefer filtered light, high humidity, and a soft bed of plain sphagnum moss packed sufficiently tightly around their roots so no air pockets remain. Watering calatheas is a tricky business. Since the moss tends to retain water, drinks needn't come often. But don't forget the chore entirely—check the moss every few days for signs of dryness. In this case, a glance isn't sufficient. Sphagnum is pale in color, and it's difficult to detect when the surface is dry by a quick look. Test for moisture with your finger, and water before the moss dries out completely.

Sphagnum moss doesn't furnish nutrients, but marantas and calatheas prefer a lean diet. Feeding once a month with 20-20-20 is sufficient in spring, summer, and early fall. In winter, many calatheas slip into semidormancy. Don't fertilize at all during their lull.

Marantas and calatheas seldom need repotting. Cram the roots into the smallest pot you can manage—the plant will reward you with a burst of exuberant growth. Although I harbor a confessed prejudice toward clay containers for most plants, I can't push terra-cotta for calatheas and marantas. They don't seem to care one way or the other—pot them in clay or plastic or whatever suits your fancy.

Calatheas never suffer in silence. They waste no time before complaining if they're overwatered, underwatered, or deprived of humidity. First the leaf tips brown, then the edges follow suit, and finally rust spots appear throughout the leaf. If any of those symptoms occur, chances are that lack of humidity is the culprit, but keep an eye on your watering schedule as well. And while raising the humidity and serving drinks, don't hesitate to splash some water around. The leaves benefit from a little extra hosing down if the spritzing is accomplished early in the day.

All marantas and calatheas send their leaves sprouting directly from underground tubers. Although cuttings can be taken, the most successful propagation method is division. Divide the crowns when new growth is just emerging and keep the humidity extremely high while the fledgling offshoots are establishing roots. Although stray tubers form along the roots like potatoes, it's fruitless to dig and plant them if they're not brandishing new growth.

For some reason, red spider mites are inordinately fond of marantas and calatheas. To prevent the problem, bring the plant to the sink regularly and douse its foliage with a cold stream of water.

Phalaenopsis

Whenever we want to give the old place a feeling of grandeur, we sit a phalaenopsis orchid on the windowsill. Suddenly the wallpaper no longer looks faded and the carpet doesn't seem threadbare. When a moth orchid is in the room, all eyes are on its blossoms.

Apparently, others have caught wind of our little trick, because every glossy decorating magazine features at least half a dozen well-heeled rooms with phalaenopsis orchids tucked somewhere in the scene. Of course, those orchids probably aren't hiding any sins, but they definitely enhance the view.

Actually, orchids have been used for much more than mere cover-ups. In the past, the presence of an orchid in a room inferred that the owner possessed impeccably good taste, quite a bit of wealth, and some gardening ability as well. Nowadays that isn't necessarily so. True, orchids will always be slightly more expensive than other plants—after all, a couple of years intervene between the moment seedlings come out of a flask and the day they finally flower. But thanks to tissue culture laboratories, you need no longer take out a second mortgage to afford a blooming-size phalaenopsis. The price went down, our inhibitions slowly dissipated, and the truth came out: Anyone with a well-lit, west-facing sill and a modicum of humidity can grow a moth orchid. Of course, there are still expensive phalaenopsis to be had if you're dying to spend some money. Breeders buy and sell quite pricey stud plants with immense petals or unique coloration. Fortunately, most of us can't tell the difference between a thousand-dollar moth orchid and its twenty-dollar counterpart. As long as the blossoms are three to four inches wide with thick, waxy, rounded, overlapping petals, we're happy.

White has always been and probably always will be the favored color in phalaenopsis. Even the so-called whites are not actually monochromatic: Their pearly blossoms are offset by either a jutting yellow or pink lip. Of all the moths, white hybrids are the most floriferous, producing ten or more blossoms per spike, which explains, in part, their overwhelming popularity.

Trailing the white hybrids in popularity are candy-striped, pink, and yellow moth orchids, all of which may be dusted with a muted speckling of pink or yellow. Although you gain more color with these hybrids, you lose impact—the flowers aren't as large or densely packed in a spray as the whites. Smaller and sparser still are the novelty types, with flashy-colored barred petals. Somehow they lack the majesty of the more understated hybrids.

There is something quite swank about a moth orchid in bloom. Phalaenopsis really do resemble a swarm of quivering moths in flight, especially when the plants reach maturity and send forth lengthy spikes stretching a yard or more into the air. The flat, tonguelike leaves are nothing to boast about, but who dwells on leaves when there are those fabulous blossoms to admire? The flowers come once or twice a year in winter, spring, and early summer, pausing for a period in late summer and early autumn. And each bloom lasts several weeks or months. The sprays usually need support when they begin to add length—special looped stakes are sold just to uphold elongated moth orchid spikes, but plain foot-long bamboo stakes with a securing twist-tie will do in a pinch.

Nine times out of ten, the phalaenopsis in magazine photos are just props. Have you noticed that they're rarely stationed anywhere near a light source? The positioning might be great for styling, but it gives everyone the wrong impression of an orchid's light preferences. If that poor orchid remains where it's been staged, it won't last long. To keep a phalaenopsis healthy and blooming, you'll need between 1,000 and 1,200 footcandles of light, which most east- or west-facing windows will supply. Don't try to be a generous host and increase the amount of light—in their native jungles, moth orchids are shaded by a canopy of broad leaves; their foliage burns rapidly in direct sun.

When it comes to heat, phalaenopsis prefer to be pampered, which might explain their reputation as a millionaire's hobby. They'll suffer if subjected to prolonged exposure to temperatures below 65 degrees Fahrenheit at night. In spring and autumn, nighttime temperatures are particularly crucial. For the sake of the orchids, furnaces are often pressed into service after the heating season has normally ended. In the daytime, moths prefer a ten-degree rise in temperature—75 to 80 degrees is ideal.

If they had their druthers, moth orchids would luxuriate in 70 percent humidity. But they'll survive just fine with humidity levels of 50 percent, which is not difficult to achieve with a humidifier in the

Phalaenopsis come in a wide range of colors, but the white varieties form the longest chains of large moth-shaped flowers.

average home. Misting helps slightly, especially if you can spritz the aerial roots both morning and evening.

Now we come to the tricky part. If a novice fails with phalaenopsis, it's usually because of over- or underwatering. Unfortunately, there are no hard-and-fast rules to guide beginners. The amount of water that a moth orchid requires depends on the weather, the humidity, and the medium in which it is grown. Phalaenopsis abhor both soggy and very dry conditions underfoot. If you must err, lean toward the damper side of these two extremes. Phalaenopsis roots are usually tucked into fir bark or sphagnum moss. And even experts have difficulty discerning from a glance when bark or moss is dry beneath the surface. To decide whether or not to fetch a watering can, dig your finger into the medium and feel for moisture an inch down. During the winter, most homegrown moth orchids require water only once a week. In the summer, drinks will probably be needed three times weekly. When the plant is dry, water it thoroughly, taking pains to keep the foliage dry to prevent foliar disease.

Although some orchids are perfectly happy in plastic, phalaenopsis need clay containers to prevent root rot. Years ago, a famed orchid grower told me his secret to success: He repots frequently in shallow but broad pots to appease the roots' desire to spread out. His advice hasn't failed me, but I make sure to repot only when the plant is making active root growth. It's fairly easy to tell when growth is in progress—healthy phalaenopsis roots look like thick worms with shimmering white flesh; during growth spurts, the tips are green. When repotting time arrives, clean the old medium from the roots and remove any damaged parts entirely, then tuck the roots gingerly (they break easily) into their new home. Since root rot is such a problem with phalaenopsis, I use only brand-new pots to be absolutely sure that infection is not spread.

Although my orchid expert friend was willing to share his rule of thumb on pot size and repotting, he wouldn't stick his neck out on the subject of growing medium. Orchid growers are split into two factions when it comes to the question of the ideal medium for phalaenopsis. Some favor long-fibered sphagnum moss; others swear by fir bark. Since fir bark is difficult to obtain, cumbersome to work with, and unpleasant to plunge one's finger into when watering time arrives, we work with sphagnum moss instead.

Phalaenopsis are epiphytes, growing on host trees in their native environment, so they don't require much food. One-quarter teaspoon of 15-15-15 mixed in a gallon of water and applied once every four weeks should suffice. With orchids, overly generous feeding will get you nowhere; in fact, your generosity can be counterproductive—the roots are easily damaged by excessive fertilizer.

The only pests that plague phalaenopsis are slugs, and they do an impressive job of making a nuisance of themselves. If slugs begin to pester your plants, slug bait does the trick. Pests might not be a problem, but diseases can prove ruinous. In particular, beware of bacterial leaf spotting. This begins as a slight discoloration or mottling on the foliage and moves like wildfire to completely deface the plant. To prevent the problem, keep temperatures warm and the foliage dry.

Obviously, phalaenopsis require a little more expertise than might come into play when you're growing geraniums or cacti. But they're worth it. A phalaenopsis in full flower is a gorgeous sight. Whether your home is palatial or something a little more modest, there's nothing like a spray of big, buxom orchid blossoms to reinforce the prevailing splendor.

Rex Begonias

Other families have portraits of their relatives hanging in the front hall. But in our entryway parlor, there's a gallery of lustrous oil paintings depicting particularly handsome rex begonias we've grown. Some folks sit a small sculpture or a silver bowl in the front hall foyer to impress guests when they first walk in. We put a rex begonia in the west window beside the front door to greet visitors.

We've always been a little boastful of our begonia collection. In our greenhouses, we display bench after bench filled to bursting with begonias. (Some say we keep the largest collection in the country.) But we're most proud of a few choice windowsill-grown plants that greet visitors to our home. As everyone knows, it isn't easy to harbor a healthy, happy begonia in a house. We want to show the world that it can be done.

Despite the fact that they're not easy to grow, rexes are sold in garden centers throughout the land. Rexes are the begonias with bands and splashes of red, green, cream, pink, and all sorts of other shades dappling the leaves. You can't miss them. In fact, you've undoubtedly yearned to grow one at home. Yet rumors of mildew and browning of leaf edges may have dissuaded you from attempting the feat.

So, what's the secret of those salubrious rex begonias in our front hall? First of all, the location is perfect: There's a steady freshening breeze rushing between the west window and the front door. Meanwhile, the light comes through the unobstructed west window with just the right level of intensity. But, most importantly, we visit our begonias very infrequently with the watering can. In fact, when life gets hectic and we dash in and out through back doors rather than using the front entrance, the begonia's brilliant leaves wilt before we remember that drinks must be served. I've always felt certain that water (or rather, the lack of it) is the main determinant of success or failure with rexes.

If you've got the right spot and the willpower to refrain from watering, rexes are certainly worth considering. Flowers aren't a major factor—rexes produce only a stray blossom here or there. But the strikingly marked leaves give you an eyeful to contemplate. And there are hundreds of rex hybrids with varying combinations of stripes and speckles to hold your attention once it's been captured. New hybrids come out every moment, vying for my affections, but my current favorites include 'Fireworks', with its bands of purple and cream; 'Happy New Year', with its festive rose, white, and green markings; 'Helen Lewis', with velvety jet-black leaves accented by a cream streak; and 'Silver Helen Teupel', with feathered leaf edges and metallic-silver leaves that blush rose in good light.

The first rex introduced into Britain was a deeply textured silver-leaved species called *Begonia putzeys*, which came from India in 1856. Compared to modern hybrids, it isn't much to brag about, but compared to the begonias in cultivation at the time, it was head and shoulders above any other species. Only two years after it arrived, *B. putzeys* caught the eye of a Belgian nurseryman who purchased the plant for a huge sum and promptly put his investment to work. *Begonia putzeys* was crossed with other Asiatic species to produce a sizable brood of progeny that displayed all sorts of colorful leaf patterns. Through the years, the work has continued until now rexes feature a

—

Windows that stretch nearly to the floor can comfortably accommodate two tiers of plants. Above is grouped (left to right) Fuchsia *'Papoose', rex begonia 'Merry Christmas',* Calathea insignis, *and (on the column) a white phalaenopsis. On the floor sit rex begonia 'Lucille Closson' (left) and rhizomatous* Begonia fusca × imperialis.

rainbow of shades rarely found in foliage. I think that I can safely claim that rexes have the most fascinating and varied leaves of any tropical plant.

Rexes look particularly fetching when displayed amid a cluster of kindred hybrids, each thereby complementing the colors, textures, and shapes of its neighbors. There's plenty of opportunity to mix and match. You can find rexes with feathered-edged leaves, rounded leaves, maple-shaped leaves, and curly leaves. There are miniatures with leaves no larger than your fingernail, and hybrids that wield voluptuous six-inch-wide leaves. Textures may be felted, furry, eyelashed (that is, with "lashes" along the leaf margins), or satiny smooth. Most rexes send out their leaves from underground or creeping rhizomes, making them very compact, but a few hybrids stand upright and can reach one to two feet in height. Once you've hit upon the perfect formula of good air circulation to keep mildew at bay and frugal watering, you can collect rexes to your heart's content.

Of course, there's a little more to growing luxuriant rexes than merely balancing breezes and water. For example, rex roots expand outward rather than downward, so choose a tight, shallow container. And don't repot frequently. None of our rexes—not even the oldest, largest plant in the place—is housed in anything wider than a six-inch container. Needless to say, clay is preferable. And when potting, use a light, peaty soil, and pack it loosely around the roots. A store-bought African violet soil will do the trick.

Rexes have modest nutritional needs. An application of 20-20-20 or any balanced feed every four to six weeks in spring and summer is sufficient. Withhold fertilizer completely from November to March. A word of caution: Rexes dislike time-release fertilizer pellets with a passion.

All begonias prefer warm growing conditions, and rexes are particularly fond of toasty temperatures. Ideally, the thermometer should never go below 65 degrees Fahrenheit at night and should climb to at least 75 to 80 degrees during the day. That rise between the nightly low and the daily high is important. When temperatures remain constant both day and night, rexes mope.

For windowsill purposes, it's often wisest to choose compact rex begonias such as 'Br'er Rabbit' (left), 'Tar Baby' (right), or 'Uncle Remus' (lower).

While keeping your begonias warm, make sure that the humidity remains high. Begonias are notoriously intolerant of dry atmospheres. In our old Victorian house, lack of humidity has never been an issue. But a humidifier might be necessary in modern abodes if atmospheric moisture regularly falls below 50 percent during the winter. And never place a begonia near a hot air shaft—the foliage withers in minutes.

No matter how high you set the thermostat, rex begonias slip into semidormancy in winter. Although young plants can go through the entire winter without showing signs of a lull, two-year-old plants usually drop a few leaves during the dark season, and the exfoliation becomes more dramatic with age. Judicious watering is particularly crucial while rexes are resting. During the winter, we usually water mature rexes only once a week, allowing them to wilt between drinks. Of course, the schedule varies according to the weather—during sunny periods, we're a little more generous. And we always water in the morning, taking pains to keep droplets from splashing the leaves to guard against fungal attacks.

In March, new growth begins. Wait for the first leaves to emerge before revving up the watering schedule. Meanwhile, don't be overly hasty to pour on the plant food. In spring, a rex's young leaves are very tender and can easily burn from excess fertilizer. Wait until the leaves have gained some body before beginning to feed. Then start feeding gradually, diluting the fertilizer to half-strength at first and slowly increasing the potency.

Rex begonias are often advertised as low-light plants. True, they'll burn from too intense sun, but they can also suffer from insufficient light, which leads to mildew and fungal diseases. Rexes grow well in a bright east or west window if the light is unobstructed and the shades are left undrawn. During the dark winter months, it might be wise to move your rex near, but not directly in, a south-facing window. It's a delicate balance. When given just the right light intensity, hidden hues appear in the leaves that cause silver foliage to blush handsomely pink and deepen the contrast between darker shades. Too much light, on the other hand, causes leaf-edge cupping followed by parched spots and shriveling. At any time of year, rexes respond

—

One of the most floriferous angel-wing begonias is 'Tom Ment', which produces a continual supply of salmon blossoms amid speckled leaves.

Rhizomatous Begonias

Rhizomatous begonias are often mentioned in the same breath as the rex hybrids. First of all, they share similar cultural requirements. Although I don't want to belittle this worthy group of begonias, there's no need to reiterate the specifics of their care and culture. Follow the instructions for rexes, and your rhizomatous begonias will thrive.

Not only do rex and rhizomatous begonias act the same, they look similar as well. In fact, rexes were originally bred by crossing the gaudy-leaved B. putzeys with Asiatic rhizomatous begonia species. But there are some noteworthy differences. In rhizomatous begonias, the colors are more subdued, while the leaf textures and vein patterns are more intriguing. And the diversity is greater. Rhizomatous leaves can reach a foot or more in diameter on a plant that stands four feet tall, or the leaves can be tinier than your fingernail on a plant no bigger than four inches. Those leaves might be maple-shaped, nasturtium-shaped, palmleaf-shaped, star-shaped, heart-shaped, ruffled-edged, or curly. The veins are often outlined in contrasting colors or raised in a spider's-web pattern. Some have long, curved "eyelashes" lining the leaf margins, some have a velvety plush that's delightful to touch, and others are silky. Many of the most bizarre rhizomatous begonias are species. Although breeders have introduced hundreds of hybrids, they've scarcely improved

enthusiastically to fluorescent lights if the uppermost leaf is no farther than one and a half feet from the tubes.

Mildew is a constant problem for rex begonias. The blight begins as a slightly shiny or powdery spot that is easily overlooked. But the infection invariably spreads until it completely defaces those handsome leaves. In recent years, hybridizers have tried with some success to breed a clan of mildew-resistant varieties. But don't tempt fate. If any rex is housed in a close, still, damp environment, mildew will undoubtedly settle in. Brisk air circulation should keep the problem at bay. Also, space the plants so that the breezes can wander between the leaves. I've found that the silver-leaved types are the first to succumb, while felted hybrids tend to show good resistance.

There's a lot to learn when you first adopt a rex begonia, but you won't be troubled by pruning chores. Although most rex begonias *on the stunning foliage found in species native to Central and South America, Asia, and other tropical regions.*

Fancy foliage isn't the whole story with rhizomatous begonias—they feature spires of flowers as well. Spring is their primary blooming season. At that time, the ornamental leaves are crowned by astilbe-like plumes of small, pastel-colored blossoms. The two-lipped flower petals most often come in white, pink, salmon, and speckled combinations. Much rarer and more sought-after are the yellow species and hybrids such as B. prismatocarpa, B. ficicola, *and* B. 'Buttercup'. *All of the yellow-flowering rhizomatous begonias require high humidity and should be housed in a terrarium.*

Like rex begonias, rhizomatous varieties send their leaves jutting from creeping rhizomes. With age, those rhizomes tend to stretch, groping into the air. To encourage a tidy nest of leaves closer to the base, give the rhizome a clipping. New growth won't begin immediately, but after a few months the plant will begin to fill in.

While rhizomatous begonias thrive under the same conditions that rexes prefer, they won't protest if you fail to fulfill all their whims and fancies. If you've had trouble with rexes and yet yearn for a few fancy-leaved begonias in your windowsill, hone your expertise with rhizomatous varieties. They'll endure a few chilly nights before complaining and withstand some dark dank weather without succumbing to mildew. Best of all, they don't go dormant in winter. And they're mighty impressive in a west-facing window. Rhizomatous varieties give begonias a good name.

will form a neat natural mound of leaves with no effort whatsoever on your part, some grooming is definitely required. As soon as an old leaf turns pale, take it off.

Fortunately, rexes aren't plagued by many pests. Mealybugs are fond of hiding in the leaf crevices, but that's the only critter to bother rex begonias.

Rex begonias are a challenge, and they probably aren't for the novice. But, for indoor gardeners with some experience under their belts, rex begonias are fulfilling and boast-worthy plants. If I've peppered this chapter with a series of cautions and warnings, it's because I know and love them so well. We have an intimate relationship. In our family, we don't polish the silver with regularity and we rarely oil the woodwork. But we take great pains with our plants, especially the begonias.

Introduction

If all you've got is a northern exposure at your disposal, don't feel too sorry for yourself. Certainly, north is the least sunny exposure on the compass. Yet most unobstructed north windows have enough light to support living plants. The trick is to select botanicals that will accept heavily filtered light without looking peevish.

First of all, forget flowers. No matter how much care you lavish on a plant, the light coming through a north window just isn't sufficient to coax it into bud unless your setup is bolstered by fluorescent tubes. In some cases, a northern exposure can't keep foliage in fine fettle, either. Most of the nonbloomers mentioned in the south, east, and west sections of this book would look rather pathetic if demoted to a north-facing windowsill. Their stems would stretch, their leaves would drop, and other unpleasant signs of stress might become manifest. Instead, stick with plants mentioned in the following section. They luxuriate in low light. You'll find many possibilities from which to choose; there's no reason why a north window should go naked. Furthermore, a collection of foliage plants need not be a ho-hum affair. By carefully combining textures, hues, and shapes, the vista can be quite fetching.

Northern exposures pose challenges beyond mere design and plant selection. Even experienced gardeners tend to overwater plants on north-facing sills. It's a frightfully easy crime to commit. In midwinter, it seems as though the plants in that exposure never dry out. A week may pass, ten days will go by, and still the soil remains moist. Nevertheless, don't lose patience and let go with the watering pot. Wait for the medium to truly dry out, and then be very frugal with the drinks. Overcrowding can also lead to problems. Although the plants recommended in this section are not prone to mildew, rot can set in if individuals are jam-packed. The scramble for sunrays is tough enough without sitting plants in one another's shade. Spacing is crucial in northern exposures.

I used to think that northern windows received no direct sun at all,

Often mistaken for a fern, Asparagus densiflorus *'Myers' enjoys the same growing conditions that ferns prefer.*

but I saw the light the week after moving into a north-facing bedroom. In midwinter and high summer, the first light of dawn comes flooding through the panes unmercifully for an hour or so. On clear mornings, the rays are really quite strong. Of course, the sunbath doesn't last long and the quick shot of sunbeams isn't enough to nourish blooming plants. Even so, those morning sunrays leave their mark. They make the resident foliage lush and keep the stems of plants from getting gangly. It's definitely worth waking up ridiculously early in the morning to open the curtains and give the dawn's light free entry.

To tell the truth, I avoid the early morning rush entirely and go completely curtainless—the neighbors aren't within eyeshot and it seems foolhardy to filter such low light. Another trick is to place plants residing in northern windows as close as possible to the glass and keep turning them to expose every leaf equally to the solar energy. Every little footcandle helps.

Aspidistras

At first glance, there's nothing remarkable about an aspidistra. The long, slender, deep-green leaves blend into the scenery. Every few months a new leaf might emerge from the base. Slowly it unfurls and begins to jut upward, eventually standing two to three feet tall, flush with the rest of the foliage. Aspidistras never look shabby, but they never really catch your eye, either. Like sansevierias (the rattlesnake plant), they just sort of sit in suspended animation. If they're kept well dusted, aspidistras can achieve a simple elegance while adding a little unobtrusive greenery to the scene.

At one time, aspidistras were something of an institution. Every decent high Victorian home had an aspidistra lurking in some dark corner. Songs were dedicated to them, short stories were written about them, and every engraving in period magazines was punctuated with a plant or two. By the roaring twenties, aspidistras had become a symbol of the establishment, a target for the youth of the new genera-

In the evening, the diverse textures of Hedera helix 'Calico' *(left),* Aspidistra elatior 'Variegata' *(right), and* Blechnum gibbum *(below) are particularly eye-catching.*

tion to rebel against. Inconspicuous though aspidistras might be, they loomed large in people's consciousness.

Aspidistras were omnipresent in chilly, poorly lit Victorian houses because they're so rock solid. The plant didn't win its nicknames of cast-iron plant and barroom plant for nothing. It's claimed that they could endure smoky, dismal barrooms where the clientele spit tobacco and poured whiskey into the plant's saucer. That may be stretching it a bit, but aspidistras definitely turn the other cheek under adverse situations. Try as you might, even if you forget watering for half a month, an aspidistra stubbornly refuses to pitch it in. You don't need to fertilize, mist, humidify, or dehumidify an aspidistra. Repotting, pruning, and grooming aren't really called for either. Any temperature above freezing will do. In fact, aspidistras will reputedly endure a nip of frost every once in a while, but I've never tried it.

You can install this plant in any poorly lit north-facing corner and forget it. An aspidistra scarcely looks different if you give it full sun or no sun at all. However, in sun, mature aspidistras will occasionally (once every few years) produce flowers. The blossoms are absolutely absurd—they're like huge, two-inch-wide, ornate purple and brown buttons. But they nestle in the soil between the jutting leaves, so you're unlikely even to notice them.

Although *Aspidistra elatior* is dull by anyone's standards, there's a variegated version that's quite handsome. Known as the barbershop plant, the variegated aspidistra has long, majestic, pure white stripes running the length of the leaves. Often half a leaf is white, the other half forest green. And the foliage is broader than the plain-green version, so the pattern is well displayed. However, variegated aspidistras are slower to make progress, and predominantly white leaves tend to turn muddy brown when light levels are very low. They aren't nearly as cast-iron as the unadorned aspidistra.

More difficult to find and even slower to send up new shoots is *A. elatior* 'Milky Way'. This version has thin, deep-green leaves that stand twelve to sixteen inches high and are speckled throughout with pronounced golden flecks. Besides its lethargic pace, 'Milky Way' is every bit as stoic as the plain-green flagship.

Aspidistras are no longer easy to find. If you have a great-aunt with a grand aspidistra loafing in her front parlor, you can easily divide a section (be sure to choose a piece with plenty of healthy, live roots and a knob of new growth, if possible) and bring it home. Peg the division firmly down in heavy soil (the long leaves can flop over, pulling the roots from their anchor) and baby it during the recovery period (about a month) from transplanting shock. After that, you can give it the cold shoulder that aspidistras have come to expect.

Ferns

Like many Victorian houses, ours was fitted with a front parlor, a useless alcove designed solely to entertain guests who might be too proud or important to enter the heart of the home. For all its grandeur, our front parlor is a rather dismal room with stuffy, uncomfortable furniture and little light. It's not the sort of place where you hang out. In summer, you might find a few languid souls draped over the fainting couch, gravitating toward the coolest spot in the house. But most of the time, we tarry in the front parlor only when company comes.

Flowering plants would never survive in the front parlor. First of all, its north-facing orientation doesn't provide sufficient light to nurture full-fledged bloomers. Anyway, it's a somber place, with a conservative (i.e., drab) color scheme; happy-go-lucky blossoms just wouldn't fit in. Ferns seem far more appropriate.

Greenery is what ferns are all about. They are a symphony in verdure in all its many forms and ramifications. Their fiddleheads might be slow-growing and discreet, but there's nothing boring about ferns. They become lush and wonderful, and in the process they teach us to explore the subtleties of nature. The Victorians felt that ferns were a higher form of plant life only appreciated by sophisticated beings who didn't require the compensation of flowers. I'm not sure if I qualify on the sophistication aspect, but I've certainly become a fern fan.

Even folks who don't share my infatuation with ferns often adopt a Boston fern into their family. Easily the most popular foliage plants on the market, the Boston fern (*Nephrolepis exaltata* 'Bostoniensis') and its cultivars (especially 'Fluffy Ruffles', 'Shadow Lace', 'Leprechaun', and the Dallas fern) are so conspicuous in American homes that they rival the weeping fig (*Ficus benjamina*) in popularity.

Unfortunately, the public hasn't singled out the easiest of ferns to cultivate indoors. Nephrolepis require fifty to seventy percent relative humidity to thrive. Unlike the leathery fronds of many pteridophytes,

the foliage of the Boston fern group is delicate, especially the fluffy-fronded cultivars. And nephrolepis don't suffer in silence if you fail to provide optimum conditions: They signal distress by a browning and dropping of the fronds.

On the positive side, Boston ferns will grow under a broad range of light intensities. They can be grown with as little as 600 footcandles of light (typical of a north-facing window) or they can survive in a spot that receives 1,000 footcandles of light. The delicate, serrated-leaved, fluffy cultivars, however, prefer the lower end of the scale—too much sun can bleach them. Boston ferns and their kin are often sold in hanging baskets so the lacy fronds can cascade down. Although they will survive in plastic pots, clay is a better choice, expediting drainage and increasing root aeration.

There are easier ferns available, and many are just as fetching as nephrolepis. In fact, there are 230 or so genera of pteridophytes, and many will thrive with less light and lower humidity than nephrolepis demand. A few possibilities for beginners include the aspleniums, especially *Asplenium bulbiferum*, the king and queen fern, so called because it forms tiny plantlets on its two-foot-tall fronds; I suppose, too, that it looks something like a crown. Misting will keep the plantlets growing until they have two or three miniature leaves and can be plucked off and pegged down in moss to make roots. An equally easy relative is the bird's-nest fern (*A. nidus*) with thick, ribbonlike leaves jutting straight upward. It can endure temperatures down to 50 degrees Fahrenheit and low humidity; however, slugs seem to be drawn to its fronds with magnetic force.

Sold far and wide for its iron-clad disposition, the holly fern (*Cyrtomium falcatum*) has large, segmented fronds that form a rosette around the crown. It isn't the most fascinating pteridophyte on the face of the earth, but the holly fern can tolerate the darkest, driest, coldest conditions possible in a home and still grow unscathed. The brake ferns (*Pteris* species) are nearly as stolid but add a dash of color with silver streaks down the center of their long, fingerlike fronds. For good color, grow them close to the window and water them generously.

—

Bay windows can be plant-filled or host merely one immense specimen such as this Nephrolepis exaltata 'Bostoniensis' *with* Jasminum tortuosum *trained around the window frame.*

Although davallias are a tad more difficult to grow, their furry rhizomes are quite a conversation piece. Likened to squirrel's feet, rabbit's feet, bear's feet, and tarantula legs, some folks find the groping rhizomes that wander about and eventually encase the pot a little unsavory. Yet they'll grow easily and send up plentiful parsley-shaped fronds in any moderately humid, north-facing window. And I find the furry legs quite endearing in close quarters. Most davallias remain compact, rarely exceeding a foot in diameter at maturity, eventually becoming a network of intertwining hirsute legs.

Although they enjoy an avid following, maidenhair ferns (*Adiantum* species) can be finicky. Their delicate fronds shrivel at the slightest chill and burn to a crisp if hit directly by a stray sunray. Fortunately, maidenhairs are forgiving. Fried or chilled plants readily produce new fronds after a slight pouting period. Grow them in warm temperatures (above 65 degrees Fahrenheit at night) in heavily filtered sun and give them a heavy soil.

Staghorn ferns (*Platycerium* cultivars) have made their way into the supermarket trade although they're certainly not easy ferns to maintain. Their overwhelming popularity seems to be the result of their strange physical appearance: Staghorn ferns have antler-shaped fertile fronds that jut from a broad, flat back-plaque. They look very much like those mounted hunting trophies that used to hang over fireplaces. However if you want to keep them in good health, banish them to the bathroom, where humidity is high, the bathtub is close by (for frequent floatings of the mounted fern), and the light is diffuse.

Many houseplant growers turn to ferns out of desperation—when all else fails, they buy a fern. But you can't stick a fern in some dark corner and expect it to thrive. Even the most tolerant ferns require 200 to 600 footcandles of light, which they will receive in an unobstructed north window. They also prefer a mossy, leafmold-laden medium underfoot. In fact, many varieties (especially nephrolepis and staghorns) can survive in plain sphagnum moss if you fertilize once every three to four weeks.

Another common misconception is that ferns require soggy soil. The truth is that they detest sopping wet feet. Rather, the medium should be slightly damp—never drenched, never totally dry.

A Wardian case (the Victorian version of a terrarium) filled with adiantum (maidenhair) ferns and nephrolepis. Beside the case is the fern Nephrolepis exaltata 'Bostoniensis'.

Ferns are rarely troubled by pests. An occasional infestation of scale may occur, especially on nephrolepis and maidenhair ferns. Aphids find tender fiddleheads tempting, and sometimes a stray mealybug will come to dine. But be careful when you combat these beasts. Ferns are sensitive to many sprays, especially those containing oils. Use wettable powders instead. Insecticidal soap has proved effective against scale.

Should you desire to share your ferns with friends and family, the easiest method to increase the bounty is division. Any fern with multiple crowns can be divided. Sowing spores isn't quite as simple. They must be collected only when ripe (the spore case will open to release the powdery spores), then dusted on a mossy surface, and kept in a sterile, warm environment (70 to 85 degrees) while germination takes place. The process can take anywhere from two weeks to a year, depending on the species.

A flat of young sporelings is a stunning sight. In fact, a crop of many ferns nestled together provides gentle soul music. Ferns don't compete with their neighbors for sun; instead, the plants bask contentedly in each other's shade. If there's harmony in diversity, then there's a common theme in the confusion of fiddleheads.

Ficus

We still have Grandpa Logee's rubber tree. Of course, it's grown gangly over the years (I figure that it must be nearing its eightieth birthday by now). In its old age, the rubber tree now lives in the greenhouses, where smaller plants can modestly disguise its naked ankles, exposed knees, and bare waist; in other words, where it can loom above everything else. But it doesn't need a greenhouse. It would be just as happy in the north window of our dry, drafty front parlor. That's where it resided in Grandpa Logee's day.

The rubber tree (*Ficus elastica*) is not my idea of the perfect houseplant. It will scrape the ceiling in no time, sending up one non-branching stalk, meanwhile dropping massive, leathery lower leaves from the waist down. While propelled upwards, it produces flailing aerial roots, which scarcely add to the overall picture. Whacking it

On this north-facing windowseat sit Muehlenbeckia complexa *trained into a wreath,* Nephrolepis cordifolia *'Duffii' (middle), and* Ficus deltoidea *(right).*

back only unleashes an unsavory outpouring of latex and encourages another shoot to rush up from the very same point. No matter what tactics you employ, the plant can't be persuaded to branch. It's got a personality as stubborn as Grandpa Logee's.

Instead, we grow a mistletoe fig (*F. deltoidea*) in the north window that once housed Grandpa's favorite ficus. It endures the same chilly conditions and dry atmosphere. But the mistletoe fig looks much more pleasing to my eye. The two-inch-wide leaves are densely held and triangular. And between those handsome leaves are tiny figs that turn yellow, then orange, then red before falling. I can't find any information on whether or not those figs are edible, so I strongly advise against taking a bite.

Topmost among its virtues, the mistletoe fig is self-branching. It readily forms a handsome, full bush, and will remain two to three feet in height for years. (Figs are known for their longevity.) At the same time, the mistletoe fig doesn't require frequent repotting—the roots will happily wallow in the same container indefinitely. In fact, it's a very suitable subject for bonsai. If you need something a little flashier, there's a variegated version with slightly larger cream-mottled foliage (some leaves are nearly entirely cream) and a slower growth habit.

Window gardeners have always been attracted to the edible fig (*F. carica*). Anyone who has ever lived in, visited, or dreamed of Italy seems to yearn for a crop of fresh figs. Granted, few culinary treats are as tasty as a nibble from a tree-ripened 'Brown Turkey' fig. But alas, *F. carica* is a cumbersome specimen to accommodate in the home. It rapidly reaches three to four feet in height, with equally hefty girth. Worst of all, as soon as light levels become low in autumn, *F. carica* sheds all of those broad, glove-shaped leaves that originally won fame for covering the private parts of artists' models. In this case, when the foliage comes off, what's left is not a pretty sight. There's little beauty in the gnarled branches of a dormant fig, and since they don't need much light in the off season, I suggest you grow your tree outdoors in summer and stash it in a chilly (but above-freezing) garage, cellar, or attic for the winter.

Ficus benjamina, the weeping fig, is the most popular fig with the interior plantscaping crowd. Everyone has encountered the graceful

—

Although not quite as easy as its omnipresent plain-leaved relative, Ficus benjamina *'Variegata' has a bit more interest in its creamy-edged foliage.*

stems and willowy leaves of this plant. Five-foot-tall specimens are sold for a song on almost every street corner. People take them home, torture them unmercifully, and still they survive. They don't seem to require light, food, water, or any other life-sustaining force. Of course, if you care to provide any of these elements, your weeping fig will thank you for it. It will produce growth instead of merely maintaining the status quo. One word of caution: While you're handing out environmental insults, keep in mind that weeping figs dislike gas fumes—polluted air can cause the plant's demise. The symptoms of environmental stress are pale, discolored leaves that eventually turn paper thin and drop suddenly.

Don't try the more elusive clown fig (*F. aspera* 'Parcellii') in a north-facing window. In fact, unless you're a highly seasoned houseplant grower, don't try it at all. Granted, it's gorgeous and very tempting, with its broad, white-speckled leaves, a white-streaked stem, and green-and-white striped fruit, but it's extremely difficult to please. It sheds leaves at the drop of a hat. Changes in light levels (the clown fig wants constant intense sun), temperature (it must be kept above 65 degrees Fahrenheit), and even position can set off a leaf-shedding, stem-shriveling spree. Moreover, lack of sufficient humidity is instantly fatal for this South Pacific native. Only professionals with a greenhouse at their disposal should attempt this prima donna.

The upright figs have a number of creeping relatives, although *F. pumila* and its cultivars hardly seem like part of the fig family at all. First of all, no telltale fruit adorns these branches. Second, while most of the clan stands bolt upright, creeping figs, as the name suggests, grovel along the ground, sending runners everywhere. In the Victorian era, homeowners used *F. pumila* to cover walls, creating a parklike feeling indoors. (Heaven knows what it did to the plaster.) Creeping figs willingly and effectively perform the task with startling speed, adhering to the surface by suction-cup-tight sucker roots that can't easily be pulled free. Like most other ficuses, the creeping fig is nearly indestructible. In fact, it can be quite invasive, so be careful where you introduce it.

Ficus pumila has several cultivars that aren't quite so carefree. *Ficus pumila* 'Minima' is a smaller version, with pinky-nail-size, crinkly leaves excellent for covering stuffed topiary forms. *Ficus pumila* 'Quercifolia' has equally diminutive, densely packed foliage shaped like tiny oak leaves that cover ground at a painfully slow pace. And *F. p.* 'Snowflake' sends forth small, white-edged leaves that move rapidly but tend to revert to plain green in low-light conditions or when fertilized too generously.

As you might have gathered, there's no sense lavishing a lot of care on figs. I wouldn't say that they thrive on neglect, but they certainly tolerate quite a lot of lapses. A north window will suffice, although it won't promote rapid or compact growth. For more impressive results, try an eastern or western exposure. Temperatures can vary from 40 degrees to 100 degrees, although the plants do better at the lower end of the scale. However, even the weeping fig will perish if placed next to an air conditioner or heat shaft.

One trait that especially endears figs to the hearts of less-than-fully-attentive gardeners is their ability to survive with little water for long periods of time. Of course, humane growers will serve drinks when the soil is dry to the touch, but busy nine-to-fivers might appreciate the fact that ficus never pout when they're forgotten for a few days.

Most ficus can remain in the same container indefinitely. They just dry out more frequently, giving you more opportunity to neglect quenching their parched soil. Pot them in a heavy growing medium—the weeping fig tends to be quite top heavy, with a slender trunk and expanding crown. Either a clay or plastic pot is fine, as long as the container is sufficiently heavy to provide ballast.

Most figs are self-branching, so pruning isn't a major factor. The exception is *F. pumila*, which will need constant clipping to keep its wandering ways in check. Grooming, however, is essential to keep all ficus from looking sorry. It's best done with a brisk shake of the stem, which will dislodge any yellowed foliage and send less-than-prime leaves showering down.

Most thick-leaved plants don't succumb to red spider mites, but figs are an exception. The leathery leaves of the mistletoe fig are particularly prone to these tiny pests. Keep an eye peeled for them. The only other foes are scale—which pose quite a problem—and mealy-bugs, which indiscriminately attack anything in the floral kingdom.

Ivy

The first houseplant that I ever grew was an ivy. I was just eight or ten years old, and I wanted some semblance of life in my room. So I raided my piggybank, marched down to the corner florist, and asked for suggestions. She sent me home with a plain-green ivy.

The ivy was something of a disappointment. I set it on my desk, much too far from a north-facing window, and proceeded to pamper it beyond its needs or desires. It received more water than it ever wanted to drink; it was plied with more fertilizer than it could ever consume; it was picked at and fussed over. To make matters worse, it was checked every five minutes for signs of growth (patience has never been my forte). Unfortunately, for all the attention that I lavished over those pointed leaves and wandering stems, the ivy didn't reciprocate by sending out lush arms and legs. In fact, if memory serves me correctly, it made no new growth at all. The profound lack of light was undoubtedly responsible. And yet the plant refused to die. It just sort of sat there. Since then, I've made my peace with ivies. I've even rekindled my affection for those shiny-leaved, steadfast, tolerant wanderers.

Although blossoms might seem superfluous when you've got a confusion of twisting, twining, interlaced leaves to contemplate, ivies sometimes flower. Very old English-type ivies can send out a tuft of nondescript blossoms, but the flowers are usually overlooked. The leaves provide the main appeal. No matter what an ivy's leaf shape might be, no matter whether it's speckled with cream or blotched with white, all ivies have a certain clean-cut elegance.

The ivy of my youth was a very conservative model—just your standard, dark-green, mapleleaf type. But ivies come with leaves that might be crinkle-edged, heart-shaped, oakleaf-shaped, parsley-shaped, willow-leaf shaped, crested-edged, triangular, and all sorts of other forms. Leaf sizes vary from minute fingernail-size leaves on 'Itsy Bitsy' and 'Oak Leaf' to much larger, four- to five-inch-long English ivy types such as you might find scaling collegiate walls. With variegated cultivars, each leaf is often marked differently than its compatriots, providing an eclectic overall display.

An ivy's main claim to fame is its athletic growth habit. In fact, they effectively cover anything that might require camouflage. It wasn't always so, however. Dense ivies are actually a fairly recent phenomenon. Until fifty years ago, ivies sent out slender, nonbranching stems. Then along came an English ivy mutant that

—

Foliage predominates a north window with (left to right) a standard of Hedera helix *'Oak Leaf',* Adiantum *'Sea Foam',* Philodendron melanochrysum, Hedera helix *'Gold Child', and* Blechnum gibbum *in front.*

branched with delightful density. Modern hybrids all capitalize on this trait, known as the "ramosa complex."

Of course, different cultivars have different growth rates. Needless to say, the miniature types won't reach their destination with the same lightning speed as their lankier counterparts, but most ivies tend to be fairly fast-growing. In fact, your primary chore is to steer wandering stems where they ought to go while simultaneously clipping arms and legs that have journeyed too far.

Besides these disciplinary chores, ivies require little work. Of all houseplants, they can survive longest without a drink, although they prefer to be watered when dry. Likewise, they'll live indefinitely in the same pot. We use stout, broad-mouthed pots so the winding stems can be pegged down into the soil, where they will quickly root. Any old soil will do—the heavier the better. If you fail to fertilize your ivy, I'm sure that it would perk along nonetheless. But an occasional shot of 20-20-20 always boosts the performance a bit. Besides scale, an insect that typically attacks woody-stemmed, leathery-leaved plants, and red spider mite, a minute arachnid that thrives in dry conditions, pests are not a problem for ivies. Ivies are tormented by no diseases. In fact, the only blemish to mar the overall appearance of an ivy is when, every once in a while, a leaf turns yellow but still hangs on. Removing that offending bit of foliage is all that's necessary.

As I discovered in my youth, ivies will tolerate extremely low light levels. However, when the environment is too dim, the branches stretch, leaving awkward gaps between the leaves. A north-facing window should be sufficient to prevent this problem.

With all the free time you've gained by not having to fuss over your ivies, you might want to try training those pliable ramblers onto topiary forms. Ivy is one of the easiest plants to train on moss-stuffed topiary forms or along the wires of a globe- or heart-shaped frame. There's nothing to it. Just plant a few sprigs in the moss or soil below the frame and begin guiding the stems where you wish them to travel. Constant vigilance is necessary to weave all the stems in. You'll have a finished masterpiece in three to five months, depending on how complex and large the frame is.

‐

Many of the newer ivies have exceptionally interesting foliage; Hedera helix *'Calico' is an excellent example.*

If you become seriously smitten with ivies, you might find yourself succumbing to a new generation of variegated, white-hearted varieties that display only a smattering of green in each leaf. They're stunning plants, with ruffled edges, closely held leaves, varicolored patterns, and names such as 'Inglebert', 'Stiff Newberg', and 'Calico'. But they require a tad more light than other members of the clan. For best results, furnish the heavily variegated ivies with an east or west window, or give them the benefit of a very well lit northern exposure.

Philodendrons

I tend to snicker at philodendrons. My mother grew a few; so did everyone else on the block. They greeted you in banks, doctor's waiting rooms, the school lobby, and in my father's office. In fact, everywhere you went, there they were, draped around spots where the sun never penetrated, filling space in a nondescript sort of way. Just as aspidistras aroused contempt in the twenties, philodendrons were targets of scorn for our generation.

Although I left my rebellious years behind long ago, I still throw an occasional slur in the philodendrons' general direction. Take the omnipresent, overexposed, poorly treated *Philodendron scandens* subsp. *oxycardium*, for example. When I was growing up, they called that heart-leaved plant *P. cordatum*, and it gathered dust everywhere you turned. Like the aspidistra, the heart-leaved philodendron is both indestructible and unexciting. With no great haste, thick stems roam around, sending out leathery leaves and caterpillar-thick aerial roots. It looks like a slow-paced version of English ivy. *Philodendron scandens* subsp. *oxycardium* requires little water (but will also endure too much, if that's your penchant), it needs no fertilizer, and any old soil will suffice.

I prefer philodendrons with panache. *Philodendron melanochrysum* (formerly *P. andreanum*) is a totally different animal than the placid little climbers of my childhood. Even in its juvenile state, the leaves are not easy to overlook: They spread at least four inches wide, forming chubby hearts with a thin central creamy streak. As time marches

The crocodile-patterned foliage of Philodendron verrucosum *adds intrigue where flowers are scarce.*

on, *P. melanochrysum* becomes all the more ravishing as the satiny black leaves stretch two feet or longer and the creamy veins become more prominent.

Often called the velour plant, *P. melanochrysum* doesn't look like your run-of-the-mill philodendron, and it doesn't act like its complacent kin, either. A native of Colombia, it prefers comfortably warm temperatures. The thermostat shouldn't go below 65 to 70 degrees Fahrenheit at night, and there should be a 10-degree rise during the day. The tricky part is to keep the humidity high while the furnace is laboring—*P. melanochrysum* prefers 60 percent humidity, which can be difficult to provide in the average home. Misting helps slightly, and keeps the aerial roots plump and climbing. The velour plant also appreciates a sturdy slab of wood to support its aerial roots and abet its upward journey. We anchor the plant in sphagnum moss and fertilize every two to three weeks to compensate for the lack of food in the medium. However, a very light, friable potting mixture of leaf-mold and peat moss also works well.

Another riveting philodendron is *P. radiatum*, which has only slightly cleft leaves in its juvenile state but becomes sharply skeletonized at maturity. You'd have a tough time slipping this jolly green giant into some obscure corner—each leaf extends two feet or more from edge to edge, looking something like a series of immense ribcages suspended in air. Although the leaves monopolize quite a bit of space, the stems are slow-growing.

Equally intriguing is the hybrid between *P. pedatum* var. *palmasectum* and *P. squamiferum* known as 'Florida Compacta'. This philodendron features a strong, self-supporting main stem and strangely cleft, five-lobed leaves that look like someone went berserk with the scissors. Stranger still, there's a variegated version with broad, haphazard streaks of pure white, often bleaching out an entire lobe.

Philodendron verrucosum is far more difficult and painfully slow-growing, with huge, rippled leaves shaped like gigantic elephant ears. Each leaf is dark green etched with a network of sunken cream-colored veins, like streams and rivulets running through lush valleys. A little tuft of soft beige fur accents the notch where the heart-shaped leaf meets its stalk. After years of providing high humidity (at least 60 percent) and warm temperatures (at least 70 degrees), you're likely to

Monstera deliciosa, *closely related to the philodendrons, boasts a mature leaf two to three feet long—a far cry from its meek juvenile form.*

have only a single pair of leaves to show for your efforts. And *P. verrucosum* is by no means as tolerant of overwatering as the rest of the clan. It prefers to be moistened only when its mossy medium is slightly dry to the touch.

If you're weary of the heart-shaped theme, try the fiddle-leaf philodendron, *P. bipennifolium* (known as *P. panduraeforme* when I was a kid). This family member is the only one from my childhood to leave me with a vivid memory. I can see it now, robustly running up its fir slab, thickly clad in six- to seven-inch-long, shiny, deep-green leaves. In my opinion, they weren't shaped like fiddles at all—instead I saw them as primitive faces, each with a long snout and two flapping ears. *Philodendron bipennifolium* was sold at every supermarket, but that didn't alter my fascination with the plant. It's still easy to obtain.

Most people mistakenly assume that monsteras are bonafide philodendrons. But in fact they are closely related—the handsomest and most windowsill-worthy monstera, *M. deliciosa*, was previously classified as *P. pertusum*. *Monstera deliciosa* is known far and wide as the Swiss cheese plant, a common name that refers to the random holes that slash the juvenile leaves. At maturity, the leaves gain grandeur and become more uniformly cleft, looking something like densely packed palm leaves. They exude the very essence of the jungle. To add to the intrigue, huge, scented blossoms stud this upscale vine throughout the winter.

Both philodendrons and monsteras are members of the Araceae, or jack-in-the-pulpit family. In their native jungles, adult plants produce calla-lily-like blossoms as they clamber over their neighbors in a rush to reach the jungle canopy. But potted philodendrons scarcely resemble their wild-growing ancestors. They aren't as energetic, and they don't put on the same floral performance either. Sitting sedately in the north window of your living room, philodendrons rarely flower.

Most philodendrons are totally pest- and problem-free, a trait that especially endeared these plants to my mother and all the other housewives of the sixties. However, slugs sometimes come and graze, defacing the leaves and ruining the symmetry of the plant. Besides keeping an eye peeled for slugs, you're only chore will be a weekly watering (philodendrons aren't heavy drinkers), a monthly feeding if you're so inclined, and an occasional wipe with the dust rag to keep the foliage spotless. In their juvenile stages, philodendrons might have a yellow leaf now and then which should be whisked away before it mars the view. Mature plants rarely shed foliage.

One word of caution: Philodendrons are poisonous. In fact, between the years 1988 and 1989, there were over 12,600 poisonings reported to emergency centers around this country, making philodendrons the leading cause of plant-related toxicity. Of course, the prevalence of philodendrons is partly to blame—the plants appear in living rooms throughout the land, within easy reach of omnivorous toddlers. Lack of education also contributes to the problem—florists and garden centers have done a fairly good job of hushing up the poisonous attributes of their best-selling product. It helps to be aware of the symptoms. Since these are very dramatic, philodendron poisoning is easy to diagnose. The plants contain calcium oxalate raphides, which cause immediate pain, redness, and swelling of the throat when ingested. The discomfort is acute but rarely serious, and seldom results in obstruction of the air passages. Still, not many parents of toddlers would want to take the risk.

Foliage Plants

Let's face it. Northerly windows just don't harbor the most fascinating plants in the world. Blame it on the lack of blossoms or the profusion of leaves or both, but most plants capable of proliferating under low-light conditions tend to blend into the woodwork. Yet there are plenty of interesting subjects out there to tuck in the recesses of your poorest lit exposure.

This chapter provides a quick survey of low-light survivors. I don't really mean to give foliage plants short shrift here. But because they all share similar cultural requirements, it makes sense to profile foliage plants together.

Foliage plants tend to be rock solid. The folks who specialize in purveying such plants have carefully selected particularly stoic species capable of enduring abysmal conditions. They assume that if you have low light, you also have little humidity, variable temperatures, and a tendency to neglect your houseplants.

Of course, if you want to coddle your foliage plants, that's fine. But you can leave town for a few days and the plants in this chapter will scarcely notice you've gone. They don't demand constant drinks. Like most residents in your windowsills, foliage plants should be watered when the soil is dry to your touch. But botanicals parked in north-facing windows don't dry out as frequently as their counterparts in brighter exposures. And when they do run low on soil moisture, there's less stress from sunbeams to cause wilting. They're easy.

With a few exceptions such as peperomias and sansevierias, most of the plants profiled here become quite sizable. The majority won't remain comfortably perched on a windowsill for long—these are floor-standing extravaganzas. Even though foliage plants are rarely available in less than gallon containers, and most will stand a hefty three to four feet in height, a twelve- to fourteen-inch pot will be sufficient in most cases. Of course, you could keep repotting them as the roots expand, but pretty soon the weight of the container would make manipulation impossible. And the top growth would become equally unwieldy—most of these plants don't lend themselves to pruning. Since most foliage plants don't wilt regularly, no ill effects result if you keep their roots tightly bound.

Foliage plants benefit from an occasional fertilizing. They won't object if you feed them once every four to six weeks during spring, summer, and fall, but they won't pout if feeding is less frequent or forgotten completely. True, they do look a little more robust when properly fed. But overzealous fertilizing can result in tip burn. Remember that plants utilize less food in low light.

As I mentioned earlier, lack of humidity is rarely a problem for the foliage plants mentioned in this chapter. However, I have seen Norfolk Island pines (*Araucaria heterophylla*), spathiphyllums, ponytail plants (*Nolina recurvata*), and palms show evidence of tip browning when subjected to an exceptionally dry atmosphere. If your foliage plant is complaining from lack of humidity, then your sinuses are apt to suffer as well—you might as well remedy the situation for your own sake as well as that of the houseplants.

The following list reflects a few highlights in the realm of low-light plants:

Aglaonemas. Even among this rock-solid group, aglaonemas, otherwise known as Chinese evergreens, are some of the most enduring plants in the botanical kingdom. It's virtually impossible to kill an aglaonema, try though you might. Some say that aglaonemas don't even need a windowsill, that they can survive solely by the light of a reading lamp. I wouldn't try it. They might survive, but they'll hardly look decent. Widely available *Aglaonema modestum* has deep green blades that shoot up one and a half feet like a compacted whorl of corn. *Aglaonema commutatum* 'Treubii' is equally prevalent on the market but far more interesting to the casual onlooker. Its slender green leaves are streaked and spotted with silver.

Amomum compactum. This is a foliage plant with a gimmick. A member of the ginger family, *A. compactum* (formerly *A. cardamomum*) emits a wonderful spicy aroma whenever you brush against the foliage. The leaves emerge from roving rhizomes below ground (dividing this plant is a delightful chore—the rhizomes smell just like freshly ground ginger) and stalks pop up in tight clumps. Unlike other gingers, *A. compactum* remains one to two feet tall when grown in a pot. But, unlike other gingers, it isn't crowned by fancy flowers. I've never seen it blossom even when given a greenhouse environment and infinite root room. Dividing an amomum is not only a pleasant task, it is a necessary one—the stalks eventually jostle their neighbors into a compact mess. Yearly divisions should keep the forest under control.

Ardisias. Although I've slipped *Ardisia japonica* into this section because it will tolerate both a north window and considerable neglect, it actually boasts blossoms and berries amid the thick, indestructible foliage. Commonly known as the marlberry, *A. japonica* produces tiny white flowers in summer followed by bright red berries just in time for the holidays. The more commonly grown *A. crispa* has handsome, thick, crinkly-edged leaves that are its only adornment for many years. Finally, when the plant is quite old, it produces flowers and a bountiful crop of red berries. Both ardisias tolerate hot and cool temperatures (although they prefer cool) and low humidity. They should be tightly potted for best performance.

Araucaria heterophylla. There's a nice tradition surrounding the Norfolk Island pine. In some families, when a baby is born, a seedling of *A. heterophylla* is bestowed on the proud new parents. Every year thereafter, this slow-growing evergreen forms one more tier of branches. Eventually, the family has a little forest of trees all at different heights, coinciding with the ages of the children. When the holidays arrive, this compact pine makes a wonderful Christmas tree. However, araucarias aren't exactly care-free. Very low light will slow a Norfolk Island pine's progress nearly to a standstill, and low humidity or overwatering will cause the needles to brown. Once an araucaria has browned, especially at the tips, it rarely recovers.

Aucuba japonica 'Variegata'. Not all foliage plants melt discreetly into the background. The large, gold-flecked, deep-green leaves of *A. j.* 'Variegata' stand out. Although most variegated plants require bright light to maintain their leaf color, aucubas display plentiful golden speckling even in a northern exposure. For the most part, aucubas are a bastion of fortitude, but when overwatered, their growing tips rot. Fortunately, the calamity is reversible if you prune off the offending tip and mend your errant ways.

Muehlenbeckia complexa. Compared to the hefty leaves and stems of many foliage plants, the maidenhair vine (*Muehlenbeckia complexa*) is delightfully dainty. The foliage may be tiny, but this plant covers ground fast. The maidenhair vine sends its wiry, wandering stems groping frantically everywhere. In a month, a stem can make a foot of growth, wrapping itself around anything within grasp. In summer, minute, nearly imperceptible flowers appear, which eventually develop into equally small edible fruit. Native to New Zealand, the maidenhair vine tolerates drought, shade or full sun, and low humidity.

Nolina recurvata. The Victorians knew *N. recurvata* as beaucarnia, or the ponytail plant. They were fond of allowing its long, pencil-thin, gently waving leaves to shower down over marble-topped tables. Part of the beauty of the ponytail plant is the broad central bulb that sits half below ground, half above the soil line, spewing its fountain of foliage. Frequent increases in pot size will encourage that bulb to expand while also coaxing the crop of leaves to become longer and thicker. A venerable old nolina (they tend to live for several generations) will spout a three- to four-foot-long mane of foliage. Be careful: Insufficient humidity or underwatering will cause the tips of the ponytail to brown and split. But a few strategic snips quickly spruce up the plant's appearance, making it worthy of marble-topped table display.

Palms. Like all his friends and neighbors, Grandpa Logee kept a parlor palm in the corner of our front room. The species he favored was *Chamaedorea elegans*. I'm absolutely sure about that, because we've still got the plant, although now it sends tall fronds up to the ventilators in the greenhouse. Palms are still in vogue, but modern growers bestow their affections on the lady palm, *Rhapis excelsa*. Far more compact than *C. elegans*, the lady palm remains comfortable indefinitely in a five-inch pot, looking like a nicely kempt version of bamboo. If you want something larger, try *Caryota mitis*, the fishtail palm; *Howea forsteriana*, the paradise palm; *Livistonia chinensis*, the Chinese fan palm; or *Phoenix roebelenii*, the pygmy date palm. All of these species can be persuaded to share your hearth and home. To thrive, palms prefer high humidity and generous watering. The larger varieties grow best if they are repotted frequently during their formative years.

Peperomias. Not all peperomias tolerate a north-facing window, but the most popular family member, *P. argyreia*, known as the watermelon begonia, will. Of course, peperomias aren't even remotely related to begonias. But the striped foliage is reminiscent of the type of foliar markings that often bedeck begonias, hence the common name. Fortunately, this plant is much more easy-going than any begonia that ever set foot indoors. *Peperomia argyreia* tolerates low humidity and sparse water. However, it draws the line at damp toes—let it dry out between waterings. Other peperomias that cheerfully consent to grow in northern exposures are *P. obtusifolia*, *P. scandens*, *P. caperata* (the variegated versions require more light), *P. orba*, and the itsy-bitsy *P. rubella*.

Pisonia umbellifera. It's a pity that pisonias are so often relegated to dark corners where their virtues are barely discernible, because they're really quite ravishing when you take a second look. Native to New Zealand, *P. umbellifera* has large, broad, pale-green foliage marbled with cream. (In a north-facing window, green and white are the only colors that plant can muster.) If the plant is given more light, a pinkish tinge becomes manifest. A little light also encourages pisonias to reach impressive dimensions. In just a few years, the broad-leaved plant will stand five feet tall with an equally broad heft.

Sansevieria trifasciata. Because they never complain, sansevierias are often set beside the fireplace or in some equally dismal spot to send their tall, lean, architectural stems soaring upward. They can endure stifling winter heat, Sahara-dry humidity, and virtually no light at all. However, they will not forgive reckless overwatering. Known by such unsavory common names as snake plant and mother-in-law's tongue (long and sharp), *S. trifasciata* hails from Nigeria. Although the spe-

cies is slow-growing and rather boring, many garden centers sell equally stoic but more intriguing hybrids such as *S. t.* 'Golden Hahnii,' with short rosettes of gold-striped leaves.

Schefflera actinophylla. King among the care-free foliage plants is the umbrella tree (*Schefflera actinophylla*). Scheffleras are as simple as they come as far as culture is concerned. And they always seem to look picture perfect—never is a slender palmate leaf ragged, missing, or out of place. Native to Australia and New Guinea, *S. actinophylla* reaches three feet or more in height with a somewhat wider spread. But now you can obtain dwarf scheffleras as well as gold-edged types. No matter what their size or color, all scheffleras are equally easy to entertain. Overwatering might cause them to grumble and over-potting doesn't particularly please them; aside from that they're ridiculously easy.

Spathiphyllum wallisii. To be absolutely fair, spathiphyllums shouldn't be lumped with foliage plants. When given a decent exposure, they send up jack-in-the-pulpit-shaped flowers that look like a fleet of unfurled sails and smell like candy canes. But even though there are floral offerings to be had, spathiphyllums are usually listed among the foliage crew because they're so easy to please. And even without flowers, the foliage looks quite nice. In fact, spathiphyllums resemble hostas, which have become favorite outdoor foliage fare. The leaves sprout in tight clumps that can (and should) be divided frequently. My favorite is *S. w.* 'Clevelandii', a small-scale version with frequent flowers.

Trevesia palmata 'Micholitzii'. Although *T. p.* 'Micholitzii' is native to humid Vietnam, it doesn't require high humidity in cultivation. Known as the snowflake tree, the young leaves of this plant seem unpromising until, at last, the mature foliage begins to display wonderful cuts and windows—the leaves look something like the sorts of snowflakes you snipped with scissors from construction paper in kindergarten. To add to the image, the new foliage opens silver against the deep-green older leaves. Don't overwater the plant, anchor the roots in good, rich soil, and be sure to repot frequently.

⁓

At one time, the rattlesnake plant, Sansevieria trifasciata, *could be found in almost every dark corner in the country.*

Why are otherwise gutsy gardeners reduced to fear and trembling at the thought of caring for houseplants? It's not difficult to grow plants indoors, really. All you need is an ounce of courage and a little coaching. Anyway, growing plants indoors is not so very different from cultivating garden flowers. Most of the techniques honed outdoors serve you equally well when entertaining plants inside. Same skills, different setting.

The primary challenge is providing your indoor plants with sufficient light. That's where the windowsill varies most from the environment outdoors. And that aspect of indoor gardening is dealt with in detail in the preceding chapters. This chapter is devoted to other various but nonetheless essential elements of indoor gardening.

Chief among these elements are temperature, humidity level, air quality, and a proper growing medium. These are all your responsibility. Indoor gardeners can't clench their fists and blame Mother Nature when a potted plant wilts beyond recovery. For better or worse, indoor gardeners have control over their environment.

Fortunately, many houseplants are happy with fairly standard treatment. Years ago, we concocted individual soil mixtures for begonias, geraniums, ferns, Australian natives, and so on. Nowadays, for simplicity's sake, we've developed one soil mix to fit all. The majority of houseplants also require roughly 30 to 50 percent relative humidity, they like to be watered when dry, and they prefer nighttime temperatures between 55 and 65 degrees Fahrenheit, with a 10-degree rise during the day. In each chapter, I've revealed each plant's individual quirks, whims, and fancies. If a plant craves high humidity, I've warned you of that fact; if it requires cool temperatures at night to set buds, I've mentioned that proclivity. But those are the exceptions. Just as most people prefer to sleep at night and consume three square meals a day, most houseplants share the following cultural requirements.

—

Large windows can accommodate sizable specimens such as the stately standard of Abutilon 'Moonchimes' *flanked by* Oxalis ortgiesii *(left) and* Justicia brandegeana *(right). Below sits* Acalypha repens.

H
O
U
S
E
P
L
A
N
T

C
A
R
E

Watering

Y ou'll see the phrase "water when dry" repeated over and over in connection with windowsill gardening. It might sound a tad vacuous at first glance, but unfortunately there's no better way to describe the watering process. I wish I could simply advise all novice windowsill gardeners to apply water every three days, or once a week, or whatever. But alas, it isn't that simple. Sometimes the weather is cloudy; other times the sun shines for days or weeks. Often you have to contend with a mixture of those two extremes and water your plants accordingly. Furthermore, the weather outdoors is not the only factor to consider. Woodstoves cause plants to dry out much more rapidly than steam heat. And the proximity of a heating vent to your windowsill menagerie will also affect how often your plants need water. When it comes to watering, there's no easy formula.

So how do you decide when a plant is dry? For beginners, I suggest poking your finger into the soil and feeling half an inch down to decide if water is needed. If it feels dry just below the surface, you can safely water your plant. If you've potted your plant properly, there should be a vacant half-inch of space between the soil line and the rim of the container. Fill this space with water once and then let the moisture soak in. Wait until the soil is dry before applying water again. If you have a saucer under the plant to protect the woodwork beneath, empty any standing water immediately.

Bear in mind that hanging plants require water more frequently than their sill-sitting counterparts, and remember that hot, sunny days will undoubtedly leave your plant parched if you haven't watered in the morning. In each chapter, I've mentioned whether or not plants will forgive occasional lapses with the watering can, but humane gardeners don't try the patience of their houseplants. If possible, water early in the day to prevent a noontime wilt and to give the sun enough time to dry out the soil rather than forcing the plant to remain soggy all night.

Temperatures

Throughout the preceding chapters, I've suggested optimal night-time temperatures for each plant, assuming that the temperature during the day is at least a few degrees warmer. It's important to provide at least a 10-degree drop in temperature after dark. In Arizona and other warm regions, plants suffer when climatically controlled environments are too static; they need a change between day and night. There's no need to worry about how much higher the daytime temperatures happen to be. Most houseplants can survive quite lofty temperatures during the day. In fact, they seem to thrive when the thermometer shoots up. Gardeners may flag, but the houseplants love it, as long as you keep them watered.

Some plants, however, have distinct preferences. Camellias are a case in point. If the thermometer doesn't plunge to 50 degrees Fahrenheit in autumn, they'll never set buds. On the other hand, some plants like warmer climates. Begonias, for example, show signs of stress when the thermometer goes below 60 degrees for several nights running, and they do much better with a steady diet of 65-degree nights. But don't assume that if a warmth-loving tropical enjoys 65 degrees, then 70 or 75 would be better. Tropicals grow spindly in too much heat.

Relative Humidity

Relative humidity goes hand in hand with temperature. When the furnace labors long and hard during the winter, it robs the air of its moisture. I've heard it said that the typical tightly insulated, overheated home is as dry in midwinter as the Sahara Desert. Judging from the prevalence of sore throats and sinus problems during that season, I suspect that accusation might not be far from the mark. Most plants require at least 30 percent relative humidity to survive. If the cat's fur continually stands on end with static electricity, the piano frequently goes out of tune, and leaf edges begin to go brown, your house is probably too dry for houseplants.

Fortunately, the problem is easily remedied. Before suggesting solutions, however, I should mention a commonly used measure that doesn't work. Don't bother misting your plants. In most cases (with the exception of orchids), misting is of little or no benefit—it raises the relative humidity for a few split seconds only. You'd have to apply the mister every few minutes day and night to produce any sort of tangible results. There are better ways. If you merely want to raise the humidity in the plants' immediate area, cluster them together and grow them in clay pots. Another solution is to fill a shallow pan with an inch of pebbles and half an inch of water, refilling it as the water evaporates. Better still, increase the humidity in the entire room by purchasing a humidifier or by placing pans of water on woodstoves, on radiators, or in front of registers. This will not only benefit your houseplants' health, it will add to your personal comfort as well.

Air Quality

By now everyone in the universe has heard that NASA suggests growing houseplants to purify the atmosphere indoors. I have no doubt that many stalwart foliage plants can pull noxious contaminants from the air. However, certain less-than-stolid houseplants are sensitive to fumes indoors. Needless to say, a smoky environment tends to weaken plants considerably—they wind up looking slightly choked. More seriously, gas fumes can cause otherwise stalwart houseplants such as ficuses to drop foliage in one swooping shower. If you use gas for cooking or for other purposes, grow your plants in another room.

Repotting

At some time in every houseplant's career, it will require repotting. For some reason, many uninitiated indoor gardeners dread the chore, but it's really a very simple feat. How do you know when the time has come to repot a houseplant? With a little experience, you can recognize a plant's body language signaling that a promotion is needed. First of all, pot-bound plants wilt so frequently that water must be applied several times daily, especially in midsummer. The foliage sometimes looks pale and the plant may lack vigor. Often, the stems and leaves have increased way out of proportion to the pot size—the plant looks as if it had outgrown its shoes. However, these signals may have other causes, so no matter how pale the foliage becomes or how often the stems wilt, never repot a plant without first checking the root system to make sure that it has filled its current container.

Once you've got the hang of it, checking the root system is easy. Although it might look like a major upheaval, a quick peek at the roots causes the plant no trauma whatsoever. Water the plant, wait a few minutes for the moisture to soak in, then turn the plant upside down, supporting the soil in one hand and holding the pot with the other hand. Tap the edge of the pot lightly against a shelf and, with a little help from gravity, the root ball will slip free of its container. If properly watered beforehand, the root ball should come out as a neat, solid clump, allowing you to examine the root system without worrying that the whole thing will crumble into a mess on the floor.

If the plant is ready to be repotted, you should see a complex network of white, healthy roots. If you find a meager network of a few meandering roots, return the plant to its original container—there is some other reason why it's wilting or yellowing.

When repotting, always select a pot one size larger than the original container. Thus, a plant in a four-inch pot would move into a five-inch container; a plant in a six-inch pot would graduate to an eight-inch container (most potteries don't sell seven-, nine-, or eleven-inch pots—larger sizes grow by two-inch increments). If you are liberal with the watering can, use a clay container. If you tend to forget waterings, plastic is preferable. And be sure to soak terra-cotta pots for several hours before repotting to moisten the clay and keep it from wicking moisture out of the soil.

Nowadays, several very good soil mixtures are available at most garden centers, so there's no need to go to the fuss and mess of mixing your own. We use a medium that is composed of equal parts sand, peat moss, perlite or vermiculite, and loam. To each bushel we add a cup of bonemeal and ten tablespoons of ground limestone. The soil should be slightly moist but not soggy when you use it. First, line the bottom of the new container with half an inch of fresh soil. Then position the rootball in the very center of the pot and fill in the sides with soil, tamping it down and wedging it in with your finger or a pencil. Don't jam the soil in *too* firmly, but be sure that no large airholes remain. (If you turned the pot upside down to reveal the soil, it should follow the contours of the container exactly.) Finally, cover the top of the rootball with a thin layer of soil, leaving at least half an inch between the rim of the pot and the soil line to facilitate watering.

Always water a repotted plant immediately and set it in a shady window for a day or two while it recovers from the upheaval. If you are using a loam-based potting medium or have added fertilizers to the mixture, you can safely wait a month or more before feeding the plant again.

To a certain extent, the seasons dictate the best time to repot. Although a plant might be pot-bound, we try not to repot in early winter. Most plants don't make vigorous root growth because of the low light levels, and the soil frequently doesn't dry out because of the short day length. It's better to wait until late winter or early spring, when growth is brisk.

Fertilizing

Some plants have vigorous appetites, others are light eaters, so I've provided specific instructions for the feeding of each plant in the individual chapters. The frequency of feeding varies, but the food remains the same for all. We fertilize all houseplants with 20-20-20 formula, but any balanced feed will do. However, not all indoor growers agree that balanced fertilizer is the way to go. Some swear by a fertilizer high in nitrogen to promote foliar growth; others suggest a "blossom booster" high in phosphorous. We find that balanced feeding prevents problems that can stem from lopsided nutrition. It works for us.

Most plants prefer a respite from fertilizing between November and March when they're not in active growth. It's always wise to taper off slowly by diluting the food liberally in fall, and it's equally prudent to dilute generously in spring when feeding is resumed again. At other times of year, mix the fertilizer according to the directions on the package. Overzealousness can spell disaster. Fertilizer toxicity can result when you attempt to invigorate a plant by strengthening the dilution—the first symptoms are burnt leaf edges and dropping foliage. And never fertilize or repot in an attempt to revive a sickly plant—it would be like giving a hospital patient a huge, rich dinner.

Pruning and Grooming

Beautiful houseplants are like living artwork—they must be nurtured and shaped. Too many indoor gardeners allow their houseplants to grow tall and spindly without intervention. Pruning might cause you to lose a flower or two today, but it encourages an abundant supply of blossoms tomorrow. A few strategic cuts can make the difference between a gangly eyesore and a sculpted blue-ribbon winner.

Of course, it's impossible to give specific instructions on how to prune. Not only does every species have its own growth habit; each individual plant has a slightly different stance. Generally speaking, it's best to begin training early in a plant's career—there's no point in letting a stem grow up woody, straight, and unbranching only to cut it down and try to force it to make side growth later in life. When most plants reach a foot in height, it's time to start encouraging branching. This can be done either by pinching out the growing tip (simply nip off the new leaf bud) or by taking more drastic action and cutting several inches off the top. But that's only the beginning: You've got to continue pruning throughout the plant's lifetime. With seasonal bloomers, it's wise to time major prunings for the off-seasons when the plant is not setting buds—otherwise you may forfeit flowers for an entire year. Year-round bloomers can be pruned anytime the need arises. In most cases, a newly shorn plant will regain its good looks and resume flowering in a few months, happier and healthier than ever.

Propagation

While you're pruning, you might want to take cuttings for propagation. Chances are, when family and friends see your windowsill garden, they'll be begging for souvenirs. Some plants (such as citrus and bougainvilleas) are difficult to root; others (such as impatiens and geraniums) make roots with incredible facility. When in doubt, there's no harm in trying.

The method that works best with most plants is to clip three to four inches from the growing tip of smaller-leaved plants such as pentas and jasmines, or five to six inches from the tip of large-leaved plants such as allamandas and mandevillas and dip the cut end in rooting hormone. Slip the lower inch of stem into a two-and-a-half-inch pot filled with light, peaty soil and water the cutting well to prevent wilting. Cover it with an overturned drinking glass or put it in a plastic bag for two weeks, then remove the glass or bag. Meanwhile, keep the soil slightly moist and set the cutting in a shady window. As soon as roots begin to show through the bottom of the pot, you can safely move the plant to a sunnier sill.

Pests

Where there are plants, there is the potential for pests. However, healthy houseplants are not prone to insect infestations. In fact, if you provide enough light, proper watering, conducive temperatures, and purchase only plants that are free of bugs, your houseplants should remain pest free. But even with the best of care, bugs do happen, and that's what this section is all about.

In my recommendations for combating insect onslaughts, I've steered away from dangerous chemicals. After all, most folks don't want to fiddle around with toxic pesticides in their home. However, any substance can be dangerous if it's not properly applied. Always read the instructions before handling or applying any insecticide.

Aphids. You've probably met up with these virulent little pests in the garden outdoors. They come in an array of colors and reproduce with alarming fecundity. Their favorite feeding ground is the tender leaf tips of new growth, where they form unsightly colonies. Fortunately, aphids are easily controlled. We use Enstar II, an insect-growth regulator that halts the insect's development before it reaches the reproductive stage, thus nipping the infestation in the bud. You might also try applying Sunspray, an ultrafine horticultural oil.

Whiteflies. These pests, particularly troublesome for hibiscus, abutilons, and pentas, are easy to identify—as the name implies, they look like tiny, snow-white flies. A slight shake of the foliage or a brisk breeze will send a horrific white swarm flitting around. Fortunately, this common pest is quite easy to dispatch. Try using Enstar II, Margosan-O (a naturally occurring botanical insect-growth regulator), Sunspray, or release a brigade of *Encarsia formosa*, pupal whitefly parasites.

Spider mites. Who would imagine that such a tiny insect could wreak so much havoc? Spider mites look like little red spiders, tinier than a pinhead and yet just barely visible with the naked eye. They crawl around on the undersides of leaves and usually go undetected until the foliage is so dappled with yellow specks that it cannot be ignored. As the infestation gains momentum, the spiders begin spinning webs and reproducing prolifically, eventually causing leaves to dry up and fall. Spider mites only inhabit hot, dry environments, so a brisk drenching with a shot of cold water will send them searching for more hospitable digs. You might also try Sunspray ultrafine horticultural oil or release predatory mites, which look disconcertingly like their troublesome relatives but satiate their appetites by cannibalizing their kin rather than harming leaves.

Mealybugs. Although easy to identify, mealybugs can be difficult to control. They look like tiny wads of cotton stuck into the stem crevices and leaves, and they indiscriminately attack just about any houseplant within reach. To halt a mild mealybug infestation, touch the bugs with a Q-tip drenched in alcohol. For more serious attacks, try releasing predatory *Cryptolaemus montrouzieri*. Be watchful, though—in its larval stage a "crypt" resembles its prey.

Scale insects. Woody stemmed plants with thick, leathery leaves are not troubled by many insects, but they may occasionally be plagued by scale. A scale infestation begins as a soft, creamy-yellow bump on the stem of the plant—it looks just like an innocent leaf bud. With time, the insect will develop a hard, brown shell and reproduce until the stem is lined with its unsightly progeny. When the insect is in its hardshelled stage (which is when it's usually detected), not many solutions work effectively. However, you might try Sunspray or Enstar II. Cedaflora (cedar oil) smothers scale but cannot be applied to ferns or furry-leaved plants.

Slugs. Nothing in the world is as gross as a slug. Those slimy malefactors slither around after dark, chewing unsightly holes in the leaves of your handsomest ornamentals. Luckily for us, they have a weakness for beer. Before retiring for the evening, set out shallow pans of beer nearby your tastiest houseplants. The next morning, you will find inebriated slugs floating in the trap. It's a sorry sight, but you can seek consolation in the knowledge that they went with a smile.

Although strong chemicals can often wipe out infestations in one quick zap, organic controls are not quite so dramatic. Spray several times in synchronization with the insect's egg cycle. Spider mites and whiteflies both have four-day cycles, so you might spray three to four times at five-day intervals. If you don't achieve control with one method, combine forces. For example, you might try rotating applications of Sunspray and Margosan-O at five-day intervals to control a whitefly infestation. Check with a magnifying glass to be sure that you've done the job completely.

Fungal Diseases

If you provide your houseplants with the proper environment, they shouldn't succumb to diseases. The most important preventive measure is to water only early in the morning and only on sunny days. Throw open the window when the weather permits—a brisk breeze is great medicine.

Powdery mildew. Try though you might, you can't control the weather. During long sieges of cloudy, rainy weather, mildew can set in. Mildew rarely infects thick-leaved plants, but it can plague certain thin-leaved botanicals such as begonias, pentas, and verbenas. It begins as a barely noticeable clear spot on the leaf surface but quickly develops into a white powdery scum that disfigures all the foliage. The breeze from a fan will prevent the problem. To control a raging infestation, try applying sulfur solution.

Water-borne fungi. If your plants are blighted by blackened rings or spots, water-borne fungi may be the culprits. Unlike mildew, water-borne fungi destroy the leaf tissue, leaving only a blackened, paper-thin remnant. As you might suspect, the spores of water-borne fungi are spread by water droplets. Thus the most effective preventative measure is to keep the foliage absolutely dry while watering. Water the soil, not the leaves. Immediately segregate stricken plants at the first sign of fungal infection. Unfortunately, sulfur solutions do not control water-borne fungi.

Because catalog prices change so frequently, they have not been included in the list below. Check with the supplier before requesting a catalog.

Abbey Gardens
4620 Carpinteria Avenue
Carpinteria, CA 90313
805–684–5112
succulents

Coda Gardens
P.O. Box 8417
Fredericksburg, VA 22404
gesneriads, passionflowers

French's Bulb Importer
P.O. Box 565
Pittsfield, VT 05762–0565
802–746–8148
bulbs for forcing

Glasshouse Works
P.O. Box 97
Stewart, OH 45778–0097
614–622–2142
houseplants

Hidden Garden Nursery
1351 S.E. Briggs
Milwaukie, OR
97222–6117
503–653–8189
herbs

Highland Succulents
1446 Bear Run Road
Gallipolis, OH 45631
614–256–1428
succulents

Kartuz Greenhouses
1408 Sunset Drive
Vista, CA 92083
619–941–3613
gesneriads, houseplants

Kay's Greenhouses
207 W. Southcross
San Antonio, TX 78221
512–922–6711
begonias

Lauray of Salisbury
Undermountain Road
Salisbury, CT 06068
203–435–2263
gesneriads, houseplants

Logee's Greenhouses
141 North Street
Danielson, CT 06239
203–774–8038
houseplants

Merry Gardens
Camden, ME 04843
207–236–9064
houseplants

Nuccio's Nurseries
P.O. Box 6160
Altadena, CA 91003
818–794–3383
camellias

Oak Hill Gardens
P.O. Box 25
Dundee, IL 60118–0025
708–428–8500
orchids

Orchids by Hausermann
2N 134 Addison Road
Villa Park, IL 60181
708–543–6855
orchids

Orchids Royale
5902 Via Real
Carpinteria, CA 93014
805–684–8066
orchids

Rainbow Gardens Nursery
1444 E. Taylor Street
Vista, CA 92084
619–758–4290
succulents

Rhapis Palm Growers
P.O. Box 84
Redlands, CA 92373
714–794–3823
palms

Sandy Mush Herb Nursery
Route 2, Surrett Cove Road
Leicester, NC 28748
704–683–2014
herbs

Santa Barbara Orchid Estate
1250 Orchid Drive
Santa Barbara, CA 93111
1–800–553–3387
orchids

Shady Hill Gardens
829 Walnut Street
Batavia, IL 60510
708–897–5665
pelargoniums

Sunshine Foliage World
P.O. Box 328
Zolfo Springs, FL 32905
813–735–0501
houseplants

TyTy Plantation
P.O. Box 159
TyTy, GA 31795
912–382–0404
tropical bulbs

Vicki's Exotic Plants
522 Vista Park Drive
Eagle Point, OR 97524
503–826–6318
begonias, episcias, hoyas

Bill Voss
3805 Louise Avenue
Chantilly, VA 22021
703–742–0997
begonias

Well-Sweep Herb Farm
317 Mt. Bethel Road
Port Murray, NJ 07865
201–852–5390
herbs

Page numbers in *italics* refer to plant photos.

I
N
D
E
X

209